MW01492782

Construction |
Essential Technical Knowledge for Residential Construction in Simple Language

Author: Farzin Naghibalsadati

First Edition
ISBN: 978-1-0695328-5-5 (hbk)
ISBN: 978-1-0695328-3-1 (pbk)
ISBN: 978-1-0695328-4-8 (ebk)

http://doi.org/ 10.5281/zenodo.15825582

Disclaimer: This book is intended for educational and informational purposes only. The checklists, insights, and commentary reflect the author's experience and interpretation of construction best practices at the time of publication. Readers must verify all information with local building codes, permitting authorities, and licensed professionals prior to implementation. Construction regulations and code requirements vary widely by region and are subject to change. The author and publisher disclaim any liability for loss, damage, or injury resulting from the use or misuse of the information contained in this book. This publication does not constitute legal, architectural, engineering, or regulatory advice.

Author Biography

Farzin Naghibalsadati, also known as Farzin Sadati, holds a Bachelor's degree in Civil Engineering and dual Master's degrees in Structural Engineering and Environmental Systems Engineering. Farzin is a certified project manager and a proud holder of the PMP® designation from the Project Management Institute  (PMI-USA). With over 12 years of experience in construction and engineering, he brings a multidisciplinary background that combines technical excellence with sustainability-driven project delivery.

Throughout his career, Farzin has successfully led residential, commercial, and green infrastructure projects with a strong emphasis on high-performance buildings, sustainable site development, and lean construction methodologies. His expertise spans the full project lifecycle, from design planning and permitting to execution, inspection, and turnover, always guided by industry best practices and innovative problem-solving.

Farzin is passionate about bridging the gap between theory and practice. His mission is to empower builders, developers, and construction professionals with practical tools and checklists that streamline workflow, enhance quality control, and reduce costly oversights.

LinkedIn: https://linkedin.com/in/farzin-sadati

Contents

Introduction

Building a home is more than assembling wood, concrete, and glass, it's about bringing a vision to life. Imagine a builder standing at dawn on an empty plot of land, blueprints in hand, seeing not dirt and weeds but a future home full of laughter and memories. Much like the ancient architects of the pyramids, modern homebuilders must blend dream and discipline. Each house begins as an idea and becomes reality through careful planning, sound engineering, and skilled craftsmanship.

But here's the truth: what you don't know about residential construction can lead to delays, cost overruns, and lasting regret. That's why this book, Construction Pyramid, exists—to guide you through the entire construction journey with clarity, confidence, and practical insight.

This book is perfect for:

🏠 **HOMEOWNERS** preparing to build or renovate, who want to follow step by step of the process without getting lost in jargon or overwhelmed by decisions.

🎓 **NEW GRADUATES** entering the residential construction industry who want real-world, field-tested knowledge to build smarter, safer homes and launch successful careers.

Why Construction Pyramid? The pyramid symbolizes durability, precision, and timeless structure, qualities every home should embody. Just as a pyramid stands strong on its foundation, so too must a home begin with solid planning and understanding. Whether you're starting your career or starting your dream home, this guide was designed to support you from the first survey stake to the final coat of paint.

1

Inside, you'll find:

1. Step-by-step walkthroughs of each construction phase—from soil testing and framing to insulation, finishes, and sustainability
2. Homeowner tips, and trade checklists to follow progress on-site
3. Side-by-side comparisons of materials, costs, and methods
4. Advice to avoid the "Top 10 Mistakes" that cost time & money

This journey is both exciting and challenging. From navigating building codes and permits to selecting energy-efficient materials, every decision shapes the final result. This book helps you make those decisions wisely—without needing to be an engineer or a contractor.

> ***Narrative Vision:*** *As you read, picture yourself walking through a construction site at each phase: the raw earth giving way to a sturdy foundation, a skeleton of framing rising into a solid structure, the exterior skin sealing in the warmth, and the interior finishing touches that make a house a home. This book is your companion on that walk, pointing out milestones and helping you avoid missteps. By the time we hand you the keys (figuratively speaking), you'll have traveled the entire path of residential construction with insight, purpose, and confidence.*

So let's break ground on this adventure.

Welcome to Construction Pyramid.

What Recent Research Reveals About Residential Construction

Recent research has highlighted important ways to improve profits and sustainability in residential construction. Rajala et al. (2022) found that new home builders generally make more money, but renovation companies use their resources more efficiently. Sammour et al. (2023) showed that machine learning, especially the Elastic-Net method, can accurately predict future housing demand. Alrwashdeh (2023) found that installing solar panels in a smart way, based on the local weather and energy use, can save energy and money. Jonnala et al. (2024) recommended using Cellular Lightweight Concrete (CLC) bricks because they are strong and help keep homes well-insulated.

New technologies are also making a difference. Building Information Modeling (BIM) helps manage construction waste more sustainably (Naghibalsadati et al., 2024). Satellite images can be used to track and reduce waste on construction sites (Ray et al., 2024). Modular construction, where parts of a home are built off-site, is also being studied as a way to reduce waste (Naghibalsadati et al., 2025).

Chapter 1: Site Analysis and Preparation

Before a single brick is laid or a board is cut, the success of any residential construction project **hinges on thorough site analysis and preparation**. This early phase is often overlooked in the excitement to start building, but it is arguably the most critical.

1.1 Surveying the Land

The first step in site preparation is a **professional land survey**. This isn't as simple as sticking a stake in the ground and eyeballing property lines. A licensed surveyor uses precise instruments to map out the lot's boundaries, dimensions, and elevation changes. The survey will mark important features and legal boundaries of the property. **Accuracy is paramount**: even a small error (for example, misplacing a boundary by a couple of feet) can lead to big problems like building too close to a neighbor's land or over utility easements. Such mistakes can trigger legal disputes or costly structural changes later. Investing a few hundred dollars in a good survey is *well worth it* compared to the headache and expense of discovering mid-project that your foundation is in the wrong place!

- **Checklist**: *Site Survey, ensure property markers are located; verify dimensions against the deed or plot plan; identify any encroachments or odd boundary issues; confirm zoning setbacks (how far from property lines the building must be).*

- **Homeowner Tip**: *Always ask for a copy of the survey drawing. This will be useful for permitting and for planning fences, driveways, and future additions.*

1.2 Soil Testing and Geotechnical Investigation

After confirming the lay of the land, the next step is understanding what's *beneath* the surface. **Soil testing** tells you how stable the ground is and how much weight it can support. Different soils (sand, clay, rock, etc.) have different bearing capacities and drainage characteristics. For example, **expansive clay soil** swells when wet and shrinks when dry, which can crack a foundation if not properly addressed. A geotechnical engineer or soil testing lab can perform tests such as drilling boreholes or using a penetrometer to measure soil strength. They will determine if the soil can support a standard foundation or if you need special foundation designs (like deeper footings or piers) to handle weak or shifting soil conditions.

Ignoring soil tests is one of the **costliest mistakes** in construction. You might save a bit of time and money upfront, but you risk major structural issues later if the ground cannot support the home. It's far better to design the foundation correctly for the soil from the start.

- **Checklist**: *Soil and Site Investigation, Hire a geotechnical engineer if needed; perform soil borings or test pits at the corners and center of the planned building footprint; test for bearing capacity, water table level, and soil type classification, check for any underground obstacles like old septic tanks, large boulders, or fill material.*

- **Homeowner Tip**: *Ask about the water table on your site. If water is found near the surface, you may need extra drainage or a sump pump to keep a basement dry. Additionally, inquire if the soil is acidic or corrosive; this can affect concrete and metal in your foundation over the long term.*

Case Study: The Cost of Skipping a Soil Test, *A homeowner in Colorado hurried into construction without a proper geotechnical survey, building on what appeared to be normal ground. Unfortunately, the soil was a type of expansive clay. Within a year of completion, the house's foundation began to crack and portions of the structure settled unevenly. Repairing the foundation and structural damage cost over **$50,000**, far exceeding the few thousand dollars a soil test and engineered solution would have cost. This real-world example highlights that proper soil analysis is **cheap insurance** against future catastrophe.*

1.3 Site Clearing and Grading

Once surveying and soil testing are done, it's time to physically prepare the land. **Site clearing** means removing trees, brush, old structures, or debris that would be in the way of construction. Trees that are too close to the future house footprint must be felled and stumps removed (sometimes heavy machinery like excavators or bulldozers are used for this). Be mindful of any trees you want to save for landscaping, mark and protect them with fencing so they aren't accidentally damaged by equipment.

After clearing, **grading** the site is crucial. Grading involves leveling the area where the house will sit and shaping the ground to direct water **away** from the future foundation. Typically, the ground is highest near the foundation and gently slopes downwards (a slope of about 5% for the first 10 feet is common). Proper grading prevents water from pooling around the house, which is a leading cause of basement leaks and foundation weakening. In many jurisdictions, an erosion control plan is also required at this stage. This might include installing silt fences or straw wattles to keep disturbed soil from washing into storm drains or neighboring properties when it rains.

During excavation, the hole for the foundation is dug to the required depth. If you're building a basement, excavation will be deep (perhaps 6-8 feet or more); for a slab-on-grade, it's shallower (just enough to remove topsoil and accommodate a 4-6 inch slab with maybe some gravel below). Excavation must follow safety rules, steep trench walls may need to be shored or sloped back to prevent collapse, especially in soft soil. Always locate underground utilities before digging. Hitting a buried gas line or electrical conduit is extremely dangerous. Calling your local "dig safe" hotline (often 811 in North America) to have utilities marked is typically required by law.

- **Checklist***: Site Clearing & Excavation, Obtain any necessary site work permits; clear all vegetation and debris in the building area; set up silt fences or other erosion control measures; establish a rough driveway or construction entrance (to help trucks access the site without getting stuck or tracking mud onto the road); grade the site for proper drainage per the site plan; mark utility locations (water, sewer, gas, electric) and notify utility companies before digging; excavate to the correct depth and footprint for the foundation; provide shoring or safe slopes for deep excavations.*

- **Homeowner Tip***: Visit the site after clearing but before construction starts. It's easier to visualize your home's placement on a cleared, level plot. Check that large roots and stumps were removed (they can rot and cause voids under a foundation). Also verify that the contractor has a plan for managing stormwater during construction, muddy runoff can create problems or even fines from local authorities.*

1.4 Planning for Utilities and Services

Early in site prep, also consider where utilities will enter the property. Coordinate with providers for water supply (or plan a well if in a rural area), sewage or septic system, electricity, natural gas, and telecommunications. Often, trenches will need to be dug to run utility lines to the house. It's efficient to trench for utilities before or during foundation work to avoid tearing up finished grading later.

For example, if you need to run a water line from the street to your house, doing it right after excavation and before backfilling can save time. If the site is remote or off-grid, plan for alternatives like a well and septic tank, or solar power and propane gas. These require additional site features (drilling a well, a leach field for septic, space for solar panels, etc.), which should be laid out in advance.

- **Checklist:** *Utilities Planning, Confirm availability of municipal water, sewer, electric, and gas hookups; apply for utility connections or permits as needed; if using a septic system, conduct a percolation test (often required to design the system); map out trenches for incoming utility lines (ideally on the site plan); coordinate scheduling of utility installs so they don't delay foundation/backfill work.*

- **Homeowner Tip:** *Ask the builder or utility companies about any one-time connection fees or impact fees for utilities, these can be significant and are easy to overlook in your budget. Also consider installing empty conduit pipes under driveways or slabs now (for example, a spare conduit for running future cables) while things are open, as it's much harder later.*

1.5 Environmental and Regulatory Checks

Before moving on to building, ensure all **permits and regulations** for site work are satisfied. Many areas require a **building permit** that covers site preparation, and some require separate grading or land disturbance permits. If your site has any protected environmental features (like wetlands, streams, or endangered species habitats), special approvals or construction methods may be needed. Always verify there are no deed restrictions or homeowner association rules affecting how and where you can build on the lot.

Finally, consider the **neighborhood and access**: Will construction vehicles have space to operate? Do you need to notify neighbors about any blasting or heavy trucking? These small considerations can prevent conflicts down the road.

- **Checklist:** *Permits & Regulations, Secure a building permit (and any grading permit if separate); post the permit or lot number visibly as required; have erosion control inspected if needed; verify compliance with any environmental regulations (mark off no-go areas like protected trees or wetlands with flagging tape); set up site security if needed (temporary fencing or signs, especially if the excavation is a hazard).*

- **Homeowner Tip:** *Take photos of the site prep phase. These can be useful later (for example, knowing where your drain lines or buried pipes are). It's also fun to see the transformation from raw land to finished home! Keeping a simple construction journal with dates (e.g., "Aug 3: lot cleared, stakes set for house corners") can help track progress and serve as a reference if issues arise.*

Homeowner Summary, Site Prep in a Nutshell: At the end of site analysis and preparation, you should have a clear, level, well-drained piece of land, officially approved for construction. The key things to remember are **survey, soil, and safety**: get the lines and levels right (survey and grading), build on solid ground (soil tests and proper excavation), and follow the rules (permits and utility checks). A little extra diligence at this stage prevents big problems later. As the saying goes, *"Measure twice, dig once!"*

Chapter 2: Foundation Design & Construction

With a prepared site, we move to the literal and figurative foundation of the house: the **foundation system** itself. The foundation is the hidden hero of any building, mostly out of sight, but absolutely essential. It transfers the weight of the house onto the ground and anchors the structure against forces like wind and frost. In residential construction, several foundation types are common, each suitable for different conditions and preferences. In this chapter, we'll compare the major foundation types, walk through how they are built, and provide checklists to ensure a rock-solid start for your home.

2.1 Selecting the Right Foundation Type

The three primary foundation types for houses in North America are: **slab-on-grade, crawl space, and full basement**. Each has its **advantages, disadvantages, and cost implications**. The choice often depends on local soil conditions, climate, budget, and how you plan to use the space.

A. Slab-on-Grade Foundations: This type is essentially a single thick concrete slab poured directly at ground level (grade). The edges of the slab are usually made thicker and stronger (called grade beams or turned-down edges) to act as footing. Slabs are popular in warmer climates or where the ground doesn't freeze deeply. They're also common when budget is tight, because a slab foundation tends to be the **simplest and least expensive** option. There's no hollow space underneath; the concrete *is* both the foundation and the floor of the first level.

- **Pros:** Lowest cost (generally), less excavation and less concrete than a basement; faster construction time; little risk of moisture build-up beneath the house (since there's no crawl space); good for accessibility (can easily have ground-level entry with no steps).

- **Cons:** Little to no storage or utility space (no basement); plumbing and utilities are often embedded in or beneath the slab, making repairs more challenging; not ideal for cold climates with frost heave unless properly insulated at the edges; home is closer to ground moisture and pests (requires good vapor barrier and termite protection where applicable).

B. Crawl Space Foundations: A crawl space elevates the house slightly off the ground. Typically, the foundation consists of perimeter concrete walls (or piers) that support the structure, creating an open area of a few feet high under the first floor. The ground inside the crawl space is often covered with a plastic vapor barrier and maybe a thin layer of concrete (a "rat slab"). Crawl spaces are common in areas with mild or mixed climates, or where you want access under the house without the expense of a full basement.

- **Pros:** Provides an accessible space to run plumbing, electrical, and HVAC, making maintenance or future changes easier than with a slab; elevates the house above minor surface water or damp soil; less expensive than a full basement but offers some storage (limited height) and a buffer space.

- **Cons:** Needs proper ventilation or encapsulation to avoid moisture and mold buildup; can be a source of cold air (floor insulation is needed); creatures like rodents may find their way in if not sealed well; you still don't get full living space as you would with a basement.

C. Basement Foundations: A basement involves excavating a full story below ground. The foundation includes not just footings and a slab, but also **concrete or masonry walls** that form the basement room(s). Basements are common in colder climates (they need to go below frost depth anyway, so you get space as a bonus) or whenever homeowners want extra living or storage space. Finished basements can significantly increase the usable square footage of a home without expanding its footprint.

- **Pros:** Provides a large amount of extra space for storage, mechanical equipment, or living areas (family room, extra bedroom, etc.); easier to service utilities (plumbing, electrical) than slab since they are often routed through the basement ceiling; can serve as a storm shelter in tornado-prone areas or a cool space in hot weather.

- **Cons:** Most expensive foundation option, requires extensive excavation, a lot of concrete or block work, and careful waterproofing; takes longer to build; needs perimeter drainage systems and good waterproofing to avoid leaks; in high water table areas, basements might not be feasible or safe (flood risk).

From the table 2.1 and descriptions, you can see there is no one "right" foundation for every project, it's about what fits the project's requirements. For instance, in the U.S. Midwest, basements are common and even expected, whereas in the Southeast, many homes use crawl spaces or slabs due to high water tables and cost considerations. In parts of Texas and the South with very stable soil, slab-on-grade is almost universal for its simplicity. Always consider **local practice**, which often evolves for good reason (climate, soil, tradition), but also weigh your personal needs (do you want that basement rec room?) and budget.

Table 2.1. Comparison of Residential Foundation Types

Foundation Type	Typical Features	Approx. Cost Range	Best Suited For	Challenges
Slab-on-Grade	4-6″ thick concrete slab, thicker edges; plumbing embedded; poured at ground level.	$5k, $15k (for average home slab, varies by size & region)	Budget-sensitive builds; warm climates; level sites.	Little access to repair utilities; can crack if soil is unstable or freezes; low elevation (watch drainage).
Crawl Space	Perimeter footing and short walls (or piers); house floor elevated 2-4′ above ground; vented or encapsulated space.	$8k, $20k (including joists/floor framing over the crawl)	Areas with minor flooding; where utility access is needed; moderate climates.	Must prevent moisture issues (vents or encapsulation); requires insulation; limited height usage.
Basement	Full-depth (7-8′ or more) concrete or block walls; concrete floor slab; requires staircase for access.	$20k, $50k+ (depends on size/depth; essentially building an extra floor)	Cold climates (frost line below 3′); needing extra living space; higher-end builds.	Highest cost; need sump pump/drainage in wet areas; longer build time; structural engineering needed for tall walls.

Note: Costs above are **very general estimates** for the foundation portion only and can vary widely by region and project specifics. They are given to illustrate relative differences (e.g., basements cost significantly more than slabs). Always obtain local quotes for accurate numbers.

2.2 Foundation Construction Basics

Regardless of type, all foundations start with **footings**. Footings are usually concrete strips or pads poured into trenches at the base of the excavation. They are wider than the foundation walls or slab that will rest on them, spreading the weight of the house over more soil area to avoid overload. For example, a common footing might be 16-24 inches wide and 8-12 inches thick, reinforced with steel rebar. The size of footings is determined by the load and soil bearing capacity (the soil test results guide this). Footings must be placed below the frost line in cold regions (the depth at which ground freezes in winter) to prevent frost heave (ice in soil expanding and pushing up on the foundation).

After footings cure (harden for a few days), the process differs by foundation type:

1. **Slab-on-Grade:** Usually, short foundation walls (called stem walls) or thickened edge beams are formed around the perimeter, or the slab edge is poured thick. Plumbing and electrical conduit that goes through the slab is roughed in place (this is critical, *don't forget a pipe, because cutting through later is tough!*). A layer of compacted gravel typically goes down for drainage, then a heavy plastic **vapor barrier** is laid to prevent soil moisture from coming up into the slab. Sometimes insulation boards are placed under the slab for energy efficiency (especially at the edges in cold climates). Finally, concrete is poured to create the slab, with control joints added to direct any cracking. The surface is finished smooth. It's important that the slab cures properly, usually kept moist for a few days and not heavily loaded for a week or more.

2. **Crawl Space:** The foundation walls (or piers) are built on the footings. These can be concrete masonry units (CMU blocks) or poured concrete walls about 2-4 feet tall. An opening or several vents are usually included in design (unless doing an encapsulated, unvented crawl space, which is a modern practice to avoid moisture issues by sealing the space and conditioning it). Inside the crawl, the ground is covered with a vapor barrier. Then the **floor system** (wood joists or an engineered floor framing system) is built on top of the foundation walls, creating the first floor of the house. An **access hatch** is often left for maintenance entry into the crawl space.

3. **Basement:** This is like building an entire extra level. After footings, typically either **poured concrete walls** are formed or concrete blocks are laid to form the basement walls up to ground level. Poured walls are common for their strength and speed (forms are assembled, rebar placed, and concrete poured in one go). Block walls are more traditional and may be used in some areas or for smaller projects. Basement walls often have steel rebar inside for reinforcement. Once the walls are up and cured, they are coated on the outside with a **waterproofing membrane or coating**. Additionally, a drainage pipe (often called a *French drain* or drain tile) is installed around the perimeter at the footing level, which connects to either a sump pump or daylight outlet, this collects groundwater and carries it away so water pressure doesn't build up against the walls. Finally, the basement floor (a concrete slab) is poured, usually over a gravel base and vapor barrier like a slab-on-grade.

One critical step for both crawl spaces and basements is **backfilling**. After the walls are built, the over-dug space around them (the foundation trench) must be filled back in. The soil used for backfill should be free of large rocks and construction debris, and ideally, it's the excavated soil if suitable. It should be placed in layers and compacted to reduce future settling. Improper backfill or poor compaction can lead to foundation wall pressures or uneven settling that crack foundations or cause water problems. **Always ensure** that heavy equipment is kept a safe distance from basement walls until backfill is properly placed, the lateral pressure of earth plus a heavy machine next to a new wall can push it in.

- **Checklist:** *Foundation Construction, Verify footing dimensions and rebar per engineering or code; check that footings are poured on undisturbed soil or well-compacted soil; ensure foundation walls are plumb, straight, and properly anchored to footings (anchor bolts or rebar dowels connecting them); install any required reinforcement, e.g., hold-down bolts for seismic areas or hurricane straps; if doing slab, confirm plumbing/electrical rough-ins and termite treatment (in certain areas) before pouring; if doing crawl/basement, don't forget to form/install access openings, vents, and any required framing connectors in the wet concrete; apply damp-proofing or waterproofing on exterior of crawl space walls or basement walls; install perimeter drains; backfill gradually and evenly around the foundation, and re-grade the site to maintain drainage slope away from foundation.*
- **Homeowner Tip:** *Ask the builder for a foundation survey or "as-built" level check before framing begins. This means having a surveyor or engineer confirm that the foundation is exactly where it should be horizontally (correct location on the lot) and vertically (correct elevation, and level). It's much easier to fix if caught early rather than discovering your floors slope or your house is two feet too close to the property line. Also, keep the foundation plans and notes in your records.*

17

2.3 Foundation Curing, Inspections, and Quality Checks

Concrete doesn't reach its full strength instantly; it **cures over time**. In fact, concrete will continue to harden over years, but the first 28 days are when it reaches its standard design strength. During the first week, it's important to keep the concrete from drying out too fast, in hot or windy weather, contractors may spray water on it or cover it with wet burlap or plastic sheeting (moist curing). If concrete freezes in the first few days, it can be severely damaged, so winter pours need insulating blankets or heated enclosures. As a homeowner or builder, ensure your contractor is taking these curing measures especially if conditions are extreme.

Inspections: Most jurisdictions require an inspection at the foundation stage. Typically, a building inspector will check the footing forms *before* concrete is poured (to verify dimensions, depth, and rebar). They may also inspect foundation walls or slabs, and the perimeter drains, before everything is backfilled and hidden. If you have special foundation features (like hold-down anchors for earthquakes, or pilings), additional inspections or engineer sign-offs might be needed. Always *wait for the inspector's approval* before pouring concrete or covering up work, failing to get a required inspection can lead to costly delays or having to redo work. After the foundation is complete and backfilled, **quality checking** a few things can save headaches:

1. Walk the top of the foundation or slab with a level to check it's flat and level. Minor variations (a quarter inch here or there) can be shimmed during framing, but large dips or heaves might need correction.
2. If bolts are embedded for securing the framing, check they are in the right places per the plans (e.g., there should be one within a certain distance of each corner, and spaced per code).

3. For basements, test that the sump pump (if present) works
    and that drain lines flow. Also consider doing a "hose test",
    spray water around the exterior of the foundation or wait for
    a rain, then check inside for any sign of leaks. It's better to
    address a waterproofing issue now than after you finish the
    basement.

- **Checklist**: *Post-Foundation Wrap-Up, Concrete cured for
  sufficient time (as per contractor/engineer
  recommendation, often 7-14 days before heavy loads); all
  required inspections passed (footing, foundation wall,
  waterproofing, etc.); foundation dimensions match the
  plan (length, width, diagonal measurements to check
  square); anchor bolts or straps in place; no cracks or issues
  observed beyond normal shrinkage cracks (hairline). If
  significant cracks formed early, consult an engineer; ensure
  foundation is protected from weather if framing won't start
  soon (cover anchor bolt holes or floor openings to keep
  water out); treat any exposed wooden elements (in crawl
  space) for pests if required by local code (termite treatment
  in some regions).*

- **Homeowner Tip**: *The foundation might not be glamorous,
  but take time to celebrate this milestone, maybe write the
  date or a message in the concrete of the basement floor or
  slab corner when it's poured (if your contractor is okay with
  it). It's a little tradition that personalizes the home. Also,
  keep the foundation survey report and concrete strength
  test reports (if any were done) in your home records. They
  provide proof of a sound foundation, which can be
  reassuring for future buyers or renovations.*

Homeowner Summary, Foundations: A great home needs a great foundation. By choosing the right type for your needs and soil conditions, and by ensuring quality work (proper reinforcement, waterproofing, and inspection), you set the stage for everything else. The foundation phase is where digging a little deeper, both literally and figuratively, truly pays off. It's expensive and difficult to change later, so getting it right is non-negotiable. Patience during curing and vigilance with inspections are your best tools here. Remember, even the mightiest pyramid relies on the stones at its base.

Chapter 3: Framing the Structure (Walls, Floors, and Roof)

With the foundation in place, the construction project shifts from the ground to the sky. Framing is the process of building the "skeleton" of the house, the wooden (or sometimes metal) structure that defines the shape, provides support, and carries the load of the roof and upper floors. This stage is often dramatic and fast-paced: in just days or weeks, you'll see the house take shape as walls are erected and roof trusses lifted into place. In this chapter, we'll cover **wall framing techniques**, **floor systems**, and **roof framing**, comparing different methods and highlighting best practices to ensure a strong, safe frame. We'll also discuss framing inspections and how to avoid common mistakes that can compromise the structure.

3.1 Wall Framing Techniques: Platform vs. Balloon

Two primary methods have been used historically for wall framing in residential construction: platform framing and balloon framing. Nowadays, platform framing is the standard in modern construction, but it's worth understanding both.

1. **Platform Framing:** This method builds one floor at a time. First, the floor structure (joists and subfloor) for the ground level is built on the foundation, creating a "platform." Then walls for the first story are framed on that platform, raised upright, and fastened in place. Next, if there's a second story, the second-story floor is built on top of the first-story walls, creating a new platform, and the process repeats. Essentially, each level of the building is a platform for the next. Platform framing uses a lot of **standard-length studs (vertical 2x4 or 2x6 pieces)** and is very carpenter-friendly.

2. **Balloon Framing:** This is an older method (commonly seen in houses from the late 19th and early 20th centuries). In balloon framing, the wall studs run **continuously from the foundation up to the roof** eave line. That means for a two-story house, you'd have extremely long studs (20+ feet) going from the mudsill on the foundation all the way up to the second-floor ceiling. The second-floor joists in a balloon frame are hung off the long studs (often on a ledger). This method has some advantages in that it creates a continuous wall with fewer breaks, useful historically when lumber was plentiful and very long lengths were available. However, balloon framing is rarely used today due to fire safety concerns (the continuous cavities can let fire race from basement to attic like a chimney) and the difficulty/expense of handling extra-long studs.

Table 3.1. Comparison of Framing Methods

Feature	Platform Framing	Balloon Framing
How built	One story at a time (floor-by-floor platform)	Continuous wall studs from bottom to top
Lumber size	Standard stud lengths (e.g., 8' or 9' per floor)	Very long studs required (e.g., 16'-20'+)
Work process	Easier, each level provides work surface; simpler to erect walls	Harder, requires scaffolding; long lumber hard to handle
Fire safety	Better, floors act as fire breaks (though fire blocking still needed in walls)	Worse, open wall cavity from bottom to roof unless fire-stopped after the fact
Usage today	Nearly all modern homes	Rare (mostly historical or special cases)
Pros	Efficient, safer construction; uses shorter, readily available lumber; accommodates platform level changes easily	Continuous walls can be very straight; slightly less vertical shrinkage; older homes claim it feels "solid"
Cons	Vertical shrinkage stacking up; needs good alignment at floor transitions	Fire risk if not fire-blocked; lumber waste if tall studs; not practical for multi-floor beyond 2 stories

Why Platform Framing Prevails: Platform framing has several practical advantages. Standard lumber sizes (8-10 foot studs) can be used for each story, which are easier to source and handle. Building one floor at a time provides a safe working surface (the platform) for carpenters as they erect the next level's walls. It also naturally compartmentalizes the wall cavities floor by floor, which is better for fire-stopping. The main downside of platform framing is *shrinkage*: each platform (especially if wood framing is not perfectly dry) can compress a bit over time, and stacking multiple floors can lead to slight settling. Balloon framing, by contrast, had continuous members so less cumulative shrinkage in the walls. But with today's engineered lumber and good practices, shrinkage is minimal and platform framing remains king.

In summary, **platform framing** is what your contractor will almost certainly use, but understanding balloon framing is useful if you work on old houses or hear the term. For new builders, focus on platform framing techniques: laying out walls, nailing patterns, and how to frame door and window openings properly.

Wall Framing Basics (Platform Framing)

A typical **exterior wall** in platform framing consists of vertical studs spaced evenly (often 16 inches on center, or 12"/24" depending on loads and insulation needs). These studs run between a bottom plate (at the floor) and one or two top plates (at the ceiling). **Interior walls (partitions)** are similar but only support their own weight unless they are designated load-bearing. Load-bearing walls align with beams or walls above and carry roof or floor loads down to the foundation.

Key components in walls:

i. **Studs:** Vertical members, usually 2×4 or 2×6 in residential construction. (2×6 allows more insulation, often used for exterior walls in colder climates).

ii. **Top Plate & Bottom Plate (Sill Plate):** The horizontal 2x lumber at top and bottom of the wall. The bottom plate sits on the floor or subfloor; if it's the first-floor wall, it's anchored to the foundation (often the term **mudsill** refers to a treated bottom plate directly on concrete). The top plate ties the studs together at the top. Often there are double top plates (two pieces overlapped at corners to tie walls together).

iii. **Headers:** Over openings (windows, doors), where studs are cut to make space, a header (a thicker or built-up horizontal piece) carries the load across the opening. For example, a 3' wide window might have a 4×6 or two 2×6's sandwiched as a header above it, supported by shorter studs called trimmer or jack studs.

iv. **Bracing:** To prevent the wall from racking (swaying sideways into a parallelogram shape), builders install either structural sheathing (like OSB or plywood panels) which, when nailed properly, act as shear bracing, and/or diagonal bracing lumber or metal straps. Sheathing is most common now, as it also forms the base for exterior finishes and adds insulation value if using wood panels.

v. **Fire blocking:** In tall walls or at certain intervals, blocks are added between studs to stop fire and drafts from moving freely. In platform framing, the floor structure itself often acts as a fire block between stories.

Framing starts usually with **building the wall flat on the platform** (floor) and then "raising" it into place. You'll hear hammering as carpenters assemble the studs to the plates according to the layout (marked typically by chalk line and pencil for each stud placement). Once a wall is stood up, it's temporarily braced with diagonal boards or metal poles until the adjacent walls are up and sheathed, giving it stability.

Common Mistake to Avoid: Overcutting or incorrectly placing door/window openings. It's crucial to follow the plan for where rough openings go and their dimensions. An opening too large or in the wrong spot can weaken the wall and cause costly rework. Also, not installing enough **king studs** (full-height studs at sides of openings) or trimmers can compromise how loads transfer around the opening.

- **Checklist:** *Wall Framing, Verify you have the latest framing plan; mark all stud locations on plates (typically 16" OC or per plan); cut all studs to consistent length for uniform wall height; frame rough openings to correct width/height (usually a rough opening is slightly larger than the door/window unit to allow adjustment and shimming, check manufacturer specs); install headers with proper support (jack studs) as per plan; use treated wood for any bottom plate on concrete (e.g., basement or slab contact); check walls for plumb (vertical) and square after standing, adjust with braces before nailing off too much; nail or screw sheathing as per nailing schedule (commonly 6" apart on edges, 12" in field, but follow local code or engineer spec); install any required hold-downs, metal connectors (like hurricane ties, hold-down brackets at shear walls, etc.) during framing as they often need to be nailed into place while you have access.*
- **Homeowner Tip:** *When the skeleton is up, do a walk-through with the plans in hand. It's much easier to visualize spaces now. This is the moment to catch framing errors or make minor changes (like "that closet door feels small, can we widen it?") before electrical and plumbing go in. Changes later are harder. Also, with open walls, consider adding blocking for things you'll hang later (heavy pictures, TV mounts, cabinetry). It's simple now: have the framers add a 2×6 or 2×8 block between studs where you know a TV or shelf might go. Future-you will be grateful when you can screw into solid wood instead of hunting for studs.*

25

3.2 Floor Framing and Joist Systems

Floors must support not just our weight and furniture but also tie the walls together and keep the building rigid. In a wood-framed house, floors between stories (or over a crawl space) are typically made of **joists** and **subflooring**. Joists are repeated framing members that act like small beams, usually made of dimensional lumber (like 2×10s, 2×12s) or engineered wood (I-joists or open-web trusses). They run parallel across the span and are supported at their ends by beams or walls. The subfloor (often 3/4" plywood or oriented strand board sheets) is nailed or screwed on top of the joists, creating a solid deck. This is the "platform" we discussed in platform framing. It also becomes the base for your finished floor materials later.

Key considerations for floor framing:

1. **Sizing Joists:** The span (distance between supports) and the load (how much weight they carry) determine the size and spacing of joists. Building code span tables or engineering guidance will specify, for example, that a #2 grade 2×10 joist at 16" spacing can span X feet. If a room is too wide for the lumber size, you either need a deeper joist, a closer spacing (12" OC), or a mid-span beam or bearing wall to break up the span. Bouncy floors are a sign of undersized joists or too long a span.
2. **Engineered I-Joists and Trusses:** Many modern homes use I-joists (which look like steel I-beams but made of wood: OSB web and lumber flanges) or floor trusses (prefabricated like open web trusses) for floors. They allow longer spans and very straight, uniform pieces, which means flatter floors. They also can have pre-cut openings (or spaces in case of trusses) for running plumbing and ducts.

3. **Connecting Joists:** Joists typically rest on walls or beams. At the ends, they may be attached with **joist hangers** (metal brackets) especially if framing into the side of another beam, or they may sit on top of a wall's top plate. Rim joists (band boards) run around the perimeter of the floor framing, tying the ends of the joists together and providing a surface to attach exterior sheathing and siding.

During framing, after walls are up for the first floor, the second floor's joists are installed. Framers will stock lumber up there or use a crane for trusses. They ensure the joists are level and properly spaced, then glue and nail the subfloor down. **Using construction adhesive on top of joists** before laying subfloor is standard now, it significantly reduces floor squeaks by binding the plywood to the joist, so nails don't loosen and rub. It's a cheap step to improve quality.

Once subfloors are in, *don't forget openings!* If there's a stairway, part of the floor will have an opening trimmed out for the stairs to connect. This typically requires doubled-up joists around the opening (headers and trimmers again, similar concept to door openings but for floors).

- **Checklist**: *Floor Framing, Check joist size, spacing, and direction against plans (and that any necessary beams or load-bearing walls below align to carry them); use approved hangers and the correct nails (hanger nails are special strong nails) for any joists framed into headers or beams; drill holes or cut notches only per allowable limits (e.g., don't notch the middle third of a joist, keep holes small and near center vertically for I-joists, follow manufacturer specs for any engineered lumber); glue and screw/nail subfloor fully, spacing panels with a tiny gap to allow expansion; ensure subfloor edges break on joists (seams supported) unless using* *tongue-and-groove panels; sweep water or sawdust off subfloors if construction pauses, keep them dry to prevent warping.*

- **Homeowner Tip***: This is your chance to literally jump up and down on the structure, after the subfloor is down, walk around and feel for any bouncy or springy areas. Some flex is normal, but if something feels really shaky, mention it, perhaps blocking or an additional support can be added now. Also, check that any plumbing or HVAC folks didn't over-cut joists later on; sometimes trades accidentally compromise framing when trying to run a pipe, so a quick look during construction is wise. Lastly, consider soundproofing between floors if you want a quieter home (options include stapling resilient channels under joists for the ceiling below, or using rock wool insulation between joists).*

3.3 Roof Framing Systems

The roof of a house not only gives it aesthetic character but also must protect it from weather and carry substantial loads (including the weight of the roof materials, and in many areas, snow loads or wind uplift forces). Roof framing can be done with **rafters (stick framing)** or **trusses (pre-engineered components)**, or a combination of both.

Rafters and Ceiling Joists (Stick Framing): In traditional roof framing, carpenters cut and install pairs of sloping rafters that meet at a ridge board at the top. The rafters slope down to the exterior walls, where they typically bear on a top plate or a beam. Since the rafters are angled, they exert an outward thrust on the walls (like they want to push the walls apart). To counteract that, **ceiling joists** or rafter ties are used, which run horizontally between opposite walls, tying the base of the rafters together so the roof can't spread. These ceiling joists also serve as the floor framing for the attic or the ceiling of the rooms below. Stick-built roofs allow a lot of customization, you can create vaulted ceilings, attic rooms, etc., by how you arrange rafters, collar ties, etc. However, it requires skilled carpentry to cut all the angles, especially for hip roofs or intersecting roof lines.

Trusses: Roof trusses are pre-fabricated triangular units made typically of 2x4s (in a webbing configuration) and metal connector plates. Trusses are designed by engineers to span from outside wall to outside wall without interior support in many cases. They are made in factories and shipped to site. Using trusses can greatly speed up roof framing, a crane or crew can lift them into place, spaced usually 2' apart, and you get a consistent, engineered roof structure. Trusses come in different profiles (attic trusses can create a storage space, scissor trusses can create a vaulted ceiling, etc.). The downside is an attic filled with web members (less open space unless you specifically order attic trusses), and less flexibility for on-site changes.

For many homes today, **trusses are common** due to efficiency and cost, but stick framing is still used for smaller projects, complex custom roofs, or where attic living space is needed in a certain way.

Roof Shapes: Common roof types include **gable roofs** (two slopes meeting at a ridge forming a triangular gable end wall), **hip roofs** (slopes on all four sides, no vertical ends, more complex framing), **shed roofs** (one single slope), and more exotic like **gambrel** (barn-shaped) or **mansard**. Each shape influences framing, e.g., a hip roof will need hip rafters at the corners and jack rafters framing into them. These details go beyond a simple overview, but a good framing crew or truss manufacturer will handle the specifics. As a homeowner, knowing the terms helps you visualize what's being built.

Sheathing and Stability: Once rafters or trusses are in place, sheets of roof sheathing (plywood/OSB) are nailed on, which ties the system together and provides a surface for underlayment and shingles. It's important that roof sheathing is properly nailed as per code (just like wall sheathing) because it provides diaphragm strength to resist wind uplift. Roofs are particularly vulnerable to high winds trying to rip them off, so connections, hurricane ties at rafters to wall, adequate nailing, and sometimes roof strappings, are critical in storm-prone areas.

- **Checklist:** *Roof Framing, If using trusses, verify truss layout matches plan (including any special trusses for HVAC openings or dormers); install trusses with correct crown side up if specified, and braced temporarily as you go (to avoid toppling); use proper hangers or ties to connect trusses/rafters to walls (especially for wind uplift protection); do not cut or alter trusses without engineer approval (even small cuts can compromise them); for stick framing, ensure ridge board is of proper size (at least same depth as cut end of rafters) and install collar ties or ridge straps if needed for extra support; double check any valleys or hips are framed with correct jack rafter spacing; nail roof sheathing with correct spacing (e.g., 8d nails at 6" on edges, 12" field, typical); leave recommended gaps between sheathing panels for expansion; inspect from below for any missed nails or boards that might have split; once sheathing is on, consider getting the roof "dried in" (felt paper or synthetic underlayment stapled on) ASAP to protect from rain.*

- **Homeowner Tip:** *Roof framing often goes quick, one day you might visit and see the sky, and a week later there's a full shape of a house. Take photos of the trusses or rafters before the interior ceilings are finished, it can help locate things later (like "where can I safely add that attic storage or which truss bay can a attic ladder go into?"). Also, pay attention to* *the **attic ventilation** during this stage. Make sure the framers install baffles in the eaves if you plan to blow insulation later, and that there's space for soffit vents and ridge or roof vents as per the plans. Proper ventilation keeps your roof healthy (prevents mold and extends shingle life).*

3.4 Framing Inspection and Code Compliance

By the time framing (walls, floors, roof) is done, the building's shape is visible and it's an exciting milestone. It's also time for a thorough **framing inspection**. A city or county building inspector will come to verify that the structural framing matches the approved plans and meets code requirements. They will check things like: are the correct size/grade of lumber used? Is the spacing correct? Are there the required number of studs at corners and headers? Are trusses installed per the engineering (with no unauthorized cuts)? Is everything anchored properly to the foundation (anchor bolts, straps)?

Inspectors also look at **bracing and fire-blocking**: for example, in tall walls, there might need to be blocking at certain intervals; in multi-story houses, they ensure there's solid blocking or draft stops where required (like along the top of first-floor walls, or where chimneys and vents go through). They may also peek at the **stair framing** (if built at this stage) to ensure riser and tread sizes will meet code, and that there are proper supports.

It's common for an inspector to flag a few items, maybe a missing hanger, or ask for an extra jack stud under a large beam, etc. Take these in stride; it's their job to ensure safety and longevity of the house. Fix any issues and have them re-inspected if required. Do not insulate or cover walls with drywall until the framing (and usually the rough plumbing, electrical, HVAC, which we'll get to next) are approved.

- **Checklist:** *Framing Wrap-Up, Walk through with the inspector's eyes: check each beam for proper supports (post under it, not hanging in mid-air); check that no obvious overcuts or notches in lumber violate rules (generally, notches in joists can't be too deep, holes not too large or near ends, studs can't be over-drilled in middle without reinforcement plates, etc.); ensure any metal straps, ties, hold-downs indicated on plans are installed; count the number of nails in each joist hanger (fill all holes that the manufacturer indicates, often a source of inspector red-tag if missing); confirm fire-blocking is installed in wall cavities that exceed 10' vertically or at soffits, etc.; confirm stair rough opening and support, as well as any temporary safety railings are in place (open stair holes should be blocked off for safety).*

- **Homeowner Tip: :** If possible, attend the framing inspection or at least get a detailed report. It's educational to hear the inspector explain things. Keep the inspection sign-off sheet with your house documents. After approval, consider writing a message on the framing with a sharpie or sign your name on a hidden spot, many homeowners enjoy leaving a little time capsule before the walls are closed. Also, take a final set of photos of every wall (interior and exterior) before insulation and drywall go in. This photo log is invaluable to know what's behind your drywall, stud locations, pipes, wires, etc., for any future projects (like wall-mounting a TV or adding a closet).

Homeowner Summary, Framing: This is the stage where your house truly "comes to life" structurally. A solid framing job means straight walls, sturdy floors, and a roof you can trust. The keys to quality framing are using the right materials in the right way (don't skimp on connectors or proper lumber sizes) and paying attention to details like bracing and fastening schedules. Everything that comes later, drywall, trim, cabinets, will look and function better if the frame is true and strong. So, for builders: measure carefully, cut accurately, nail correctly. For homeowners: it might just look like a bunch of wood, but it's the bones of your home, so treat it with the importance it deserves. A famous quote goes, *"We shape our buildings, and afterwards our buildings shape us."* During framing, you are literally shaping the dwelling that will shape your daily life.

Chapter 4: Exterior Systems
Roofing, Siding, and Exterior Finishes

With the structure framed, the next priority is to **get the house "dried in."** This means installing the exterior coverings that keep water and weather out: primarily the roofing and the wall cladding (siding, brick, etc.), along with properly installed windows and doors. In this chapter, we'll discuss common **roofing materials and systems**, various **exterior wall finishes**, and best practices for keeping the elements at bay. We'll also compare options in terms of durability, cost, and aesthetics, and provide checklists for a watertight, well-finished exterior. By the end of this phase, the house will look much closer to a home from the outside, and importantly, the interior will be protected so that electrical, plumbing, and interior finishes can proceed without weather delays.

4.1 Roofing Materials and Installation

A roof must perform under tough conditions: scorching sun, pouring rain, high winds, maybe heavy snow loads, and wide temperature swings. Choosing a **roofing material** depends on climate, budget, and style. The most common roofing for North American homes is **asphalt shingles**, but metal roofing, tiles, wood shakes, and solar tiles are also options.

A. Asphalt Shingles: These are composed of a fiberglass mat coated with asphalt and mineral granules. They come in 3-tab or architectural (dimensional) styles. Asphalt shingles are popular for their **affordability and ease of installation**. A typical asphalt shingle roof might last 20-30 years (higher-quality ones can last 40+ years with proper maintenance). They work in most climates, though extreme heat can shorten their life and very high winds can sometimes lift or tear them (special high-wind-rated shingles

34

are available for hurricane zones). Installation involves nailing the shingles to the roof sheathing with overlapping rows, starting from the bottom edge (eave) and working upward. Underneath, contractors install **roofing underlayment** (felt paper or synthetic membrane) as a second layer of defense, and waterproof strips called **ice and water shield** at eaves and valleys (critical in colder regions to prevent ice dam leaks). Proper attic ventilation is also crucial with shingles to prevent heat buildup that cooks them and moisture buildup that can cause mold.

- **Pros:** Lowest cost roofing option, widely available, many color/style choices; easy to repair small areas; moderate weight (okay for most structures).
- **Cons:** Shorter lifespan than some premium materials; can be prone to damage in extreme weather (e.g., hail can bruise shingles, high winds can rip them if not sealed well); made from petroleum (not the most eco-friendly, though some recycling programs exist).

B. Metal Roofing: Metal roofs (steel, aluminum, or copper) are rising in popularity. They often come as interlocking panels or shingles. The classic look is standing seam, long vertical panels running from ridge to eave with raised seams. Metal is extremely durable (40-70 year lifespan isn't uncommon) and very resistant to fire, rot, and insects. It's great for shedding snow (snow slides right off a smooth metal roof). Aluminum and copper won't rust; steel is coated to resist rust. Metal roofs are lightweight relative to tiles, but a bit heavier than asphalt (still, most structures that can hold shingles can hold metal easily). They do require precise installation to avoid leaks at seams or fastener points.

- **Pros:** Longevity; low maintenance; reflective coatings can reduce cooling costs (energy efficient); excellent wind and fire resistance.

- **Cons:** Higher upfront cost (often 2-3 times asphalt shingle cost); installation is specialized; can be noisier in rain if not insulated well (though with attic insulation, this is usually not an issue); style, modern metals look great to some, but others prefer traditional look of shingles or tile.

C. Tile Roofing (Clay/Concrete): Tile roofs give a classic, upscale look (think Mediterranean or Spanish style with red clay tiles, or concrete tiles that can mimic wood shakes or slate). They are **heavy**, a structural engineer must confirm the roof can support them (often around 800-1200 lbs per square (100 sq ft), several times a shingle roof weight). Tiles can last a very long time (50+ years), and clay in particular doesn't degrade much at all, the underlayment might need replacing eventually, but the tiles can often be reused. They excel in hot climates (tiles breathe and allow air flow, keeping roofs cooler). Installation involves hanging or nailing tiles onto wood battens or directly on the sheathing, carefully overlapping to shed water.

- **Pros:** Extremely durable and long-lasting; great aesthetics for certain architectural styles; fireproof; resistant to rot/insects.
- **Cons:** Very heavy (may require extra framing); expensive material and labor; brittle, can crack if walked on or hit by heavy impact; not suitable for shallow pitch roofs (need sufficient slope to shed water properly).

D. Wood Shakes/Shingles: These are wooden roofing pieces, traditionally cedar, that give a natural, rustic look. Wood shingles are sawn and uniform; shakes are split and more irregular. They require a good deal of maintenance (periodic treatment for rot/insects, and cleaning of debris to prevent moisture retention). They're also not allowed in some fire-prone regions unless treated for fire resistance. They can last 20-40 years if cared for, but generally are less common today due to maintenance and fire concerns.

- **Pros:** Beautiful natural appearance; cedar has natural oils that resist rot initially; provides some insulation value and breathability.
- **Cons:** Combustible (unless specially treated); can grow moss or algae if in damp shade; more upkeep; moderate cost but high labor to install.

E. Flat Roof Materials: (For completeness, though most homes have pitched roofs, some modern designs have flat or low-slope roofs). These use membranes like **modified bitumen, EPDM rubber, or TPO**. These are specialized installations, often seen on additions or contemporary homes. Key is ensuring proper drainage (slight pitch to drains) and careful sealing of seams.

Table 4.1. Roofing Material Comparison

Roofing	Lifespan	Relative Cost	Key Benefits	Considerations
Asphalt Shingles	~20-30 years (std) up to 40+ (premium)	$ (Least expensive)	Easy install/repair; many styles; decent all-around performance.	Can be damaged by extreme weather; shorter life; dark colors absorb heat.
Metal Panels	40-70 years	$$$ (High upfront)	Very durable; sheds snow; fireproof; reflective (cool roof).	Higher cost; needs skilled install; modern look (may not fit all aesthetics).
Clay/Concrete Tile	50+ years	$$$ (High, plus structural needs)	Extremely durable; classic style; low heat transmission.	Heavy (ensure structure support); can crack under impact; higher cost.
Wood Shake/Shingle	20-35 years	$$ (Moderate-High, plus maintenance)	Natural beauty; traditional look; moderate weight.	Fire risk; needs maintenance; can mold/rot in wet climates.
Synthetic/Other	Varies (30-50 yrs)	$$ to $$$	Includes composites (rubber/slate look), solar shingles, etc. Often lighter and designed to mimic high-end look.	Newer products, check track record; some made from recycled material (eco-friendly); cost and availability vary.

Roof Installation Tips: No matter the material, roofs have critical flashings that must be installed correctly. Flashing refers to pieces of metal (usually aluminum or galvanized steel, sometimes copper) that go around intersections and protrusions, like chimneys, skylights, roof valleys, vents, and where roof meets wall. A common saying is "it's not usually the roofing that leaks, it's the flashing." So ensuring step flashing along walls, apron flashing at chimneys, and proper valley lining is crucial. Also, the **roof trim** matters: soffits (underside of eaves) and fascia boards (the face board on eaves) not only make the roof look finished but also provide attachment for gutters and help with ventilation intake (if you have soffit vents).

- **Checklist***: Roofing Installation, Verify roof deck is clean and smooth (no protruding nails or gaps) before covering; Install drip edge flashings at eaves and rakes (edges of roof) to protect decking edges; install ice & water shield membrane at least 2-3 feet up from eaves (or entire roof in low slope areas) and in valleys; lay roofing underlayment across entire deck with proper overlaps; follow manufacturer instructions for roofing material installation (nailing pattern, overlap, etc. for shingles or panels); ensure flashings at penetrations (vent pipes, chimney) are correctly placed (usually under the upper side of shingles, over the lower side, etc., to route water out); install ridge vent or other ventilation as required at the peak; once finished, check that all debris (like stray nails, cut pieces) are cleared, use a magnetic sweeper around house for nails. If gutters are part of project, ideally install them soon after roofing to control water runoff.*

- **Homeowner Tip**: *Ask about warranties, many roofing materials come with warranty, but often only if installed exactly to spec and sometimes by certified installers. Keep any excess shingles or tiles in storage; they can be handy for future repairs to match color/shape. Also, after any major storm, do a visual check (from ground or safely on ladder) of your roof for missing shingles or damage. Finding and fixing a couple of lost shingles early can prevent a leak from developing.*

4.2 Exterior Walls: House Wrap, Siding, and Veneers

The exterior walls of your home are not only about looks; they are the **shield** between your living space and the outside world. It's a multi-layered system: structure (sheathing), moisture barrier, possibly insulation, and the outer cladding that faces the weather.

After framing, typically **sheathing** (OSB/Plywood) is already on the walls. The next layer is usually a **house wrap** or building paper, a breathable moisture barrier that goes over the sheathing to keep rain out but let water vapor escape (so your walls don't trap moisture). Common housewraps are synthetic sheets like Tyvek, or you might see builders use asphalt-saturated felt paper (tar paper) which is traditional. The wrap is installed with overlaps shingle-style (upper pieces over lower pieces) and taped at seams, creating a continuous barrier.

With the house wrap on, windows and exterior doors are installed. Flashing tape is used around window openings to seal them to the wrap (proper technique is important: sill flashing first, then window, then jamb flashings, then head flashing, always layering so water sheds outward).

Now the **siding or veneer** can be applied. Options include:

1. **Vinyl Siding:** A very common, low-cost cladding made of PVC
   in strips or "shingles" that interlock. Vinyl is lightweight,
   never needs painting (color is solid through the material),
   and relatively easy to install. It can mimic wood lap siding or
   shingles in appearance. It's also low-maintenance (just wash
   occasionally). However, it can crack in extreme cold or fade
   over many years, and some people don't like the
   environmental impact of PVC or its look compared to real
   wood. It's popular in tract housing and has improved in
   appearance over the years.

2. **Fiber-Cement Siding:** Often known by brand names like
   HardiePlank, this is a durable material made of cement, sand,
   and cellulose fibers. It's molded to look like wood planks,
   shingles, or panels. Fiber-cement is **fire-resistant, insect-
   resistant, and rot-resistant**, making it a very long-lasting
   choice (30-50 year lifespan easily with good paint). It holds
   paint well (comes pre-primed, and you paint it, or some
   products are pre-finished). It's heavier to work with than
   vinyl or wood, but gives a solid feel. Cost is moderate, more
   than vinyl, usually less than wood in many cases.

3. **Wood Siding:** This covers a range of styles: clapboard
   (horizontal lap siding), board-and-batten (vertical boards
   with seams covered by battens), wood shingles or shakes,
   etc. Wood from cedar, redwood, pine, etc., has been used for
   centuries. It has a classic look and can be painted or stained
   any color. It does, however, require regular maintenance,
   repainting or sealing every few years, and vigilance for rot or
   pests. Engineered wood sidings (like LP SmartSide) are an
   option that use wood fibers and resins for more uniform,
   moisture-resistant behavior, while retaining a wood look.

4. **Brick or Stone Veneer:** Many homes use a single layer of
   brick or stone as a **veneer** on the outside (as opposed to
   structural brick which would be multiple layers thick and

load-bearing). A veneer is tied to the wood framing with metal ties and has a small air gap behind it for drainage. Brick/stone exteriors are prized for **durability and low maintenance**, they don't need painting and can last the life of the building. They are more expensive to install (material and skilled labor), and add weight (the foundation must support them, usually not an issue if planned, but can't just add brick later without checking structure). They also add thermal mass which is good in some climates (slows heat transfer).

5. **Stucco:** Common in the Southwest or in Mediterranean-style homes, stucco is a cement plaster applied over the exterior. Traditional stucco is a 3-coat system (scratch coat, brown coat, finish coat) over a wire lath. Newer EIFS (Exterior Insulation and Finish Systems) use foam insulation boards with a thin synthetic stucco topcoat. Stucco provides a seamless, masonry-like finish that can be textured. It's durable in dry climates but can have issues in very wet climates if not detailed correctly (water can get behind and cause damage if not allowed to escape). It also can crack with building movement (controlled by expansion joints on large areas).

Key principle for exteriors: Manage water. Every siding or veneer system should be installed such that water that gets behind it (because some will, in heavy rain or through tiny cracks) has a way out at the bottom. This is why overlaps, flashing, and drainage gaps are so important. For example, vinyl siding is hung loosely with gaps precisely to let it expand and to let moisture escape. Brick veneer walls have **weep holes** at the bottom (small gaps in mortar) so water can drain from the cavity behind. Ignoring these details can lead to water intrusion, rot, and mold inside walls.

- **Checklist:** *Siding & Exterior Finish, Repair any damaged sheathing first; install housewrap or building paper with proper overlaps (bottom over foundation flashing, layers overlapping downwards, tape seams and around openings); integrate window and door flashing with housewrap (follow a reputable flashing detail: sill pan or tape at bottom, sides taped over nailing flange, top taped or head flashing that goes under wrap above); for wood or fiber-cement lap siding, keep joints staggered and use flashing behind butt joints, and leave proper clearances (e.g., 6" above grade for wood siding, a gap above roof lines, etc. to avoid moisture); nail siding as per instructions (not too tight for vinyl to allow movement, use corrosion-resistant nails for all exteriors); paint or seal any raw wood cuts; install trim boards around windows/doors and corners, caulk where siding meets trim to seal gaps; for masonry, ensure wall ties are installed to studs, maintain air gap, don't drop mortar into cavity (or clean it out), and keep weep holes clear; for stucco, make sure control joints are placed per large area requirements and the base waterproofing (2 layers of paper typically) and weep screed at bottom are in place.*

- **Homeowner Tip:** *Once siding is up, do a slow walk-around inspection on a rainy day or with a hose test. Check around windows and doors from inside for any hint of water. It's easier to fix a caulking or flashing issue before interior finishes go in. Keep an eye annually on your exterior: touch up paint before it peels (especially on sun-drenched sides), and clean out gutters regularly. Also, if you ever install anything like a new light, vent, or fixture on siding later, take care to seal the penetration properly, little gaps can cause big problems over time.*

4.3 Windows, Doors, and Insulation (Exterior Envelope)

Windows and exterior doors are installed typically during the siding process. We touched on flashing them properly. To expand: windows usually have a nailing flange that goes against the sheathing. The installation sequence is:

1. Put flashing tape at the bottom of the rough opening (or a sill pan) so any water that gets to the bottom will go back out.
2. Install window plumb and level, nail the flanges (or fasten per manufacturer).
3. Tape the sides over the flange (sticking half on flange, half on housewrap).
4. The top flange either gets taped **or** a metal head flashing goes under the housewrap above it, the idea is that the housewrap overlaps the top of the window to shed water over it, not behind it. Doors are similar except no flange usually, they rely on caulking and proper shimming and flashing at the sill.

Once windows and doors are in and exterior cladding is done, **insulation** often is added in exterior walls (if not already done). However, many builders wait to insulate until after rough plumbing, electrical, and HVAC (discussed in next chapter) are done, because those trades often need to go inside walls. So insulation is kind of the last step before interior finishes. But it's part of that exterior envelope discussion: a well-sealed and insulated exterior is crucial for energy efficiency and comfort.

Common wall insulation is fiberglass batts, though many builders now use blown-in cellulose or fiberglass, or spray foam for higher performance. In cold climates, exterior foam board insulation might be added on outside of sheathing before siding (as continuous insulation to reduce thermal bridging). If that's done, it needs detailing to not trap moisture (and windows will have wider trim, etc.). It's a bit beyond scope here, but mention that energy codes increasingly call for tighter, better insulated envelopes. We have a separate chapter on sustainable building that will elaborate on high-efficiency options.

- **Checklist:** *Exterior Wrap-Up, All windows and doors flashed and sealed; siding/brick/stucco completed with all edges sealed or finished; eaves and trim done; soffit vents open if applicable; gutters and downspouts installed (with extensions to carry water away from foundation); exterior light fixture boxes in place with wires (caps on until fixtures later); any penetrations (vents for kitchen bath fans, HVAC exhausts, etc.) properly flashed and sealed; insulation in walls per spec (don't forget areas like rim joists, those often need foam or stuffing to not leave a gap); attic insulation plan in place (if doing blown later, ensure baffles at eaves to keep soffit vents clear); caulking done where needed. At this stage, essentially the building should be able to keep the weather out and hold temperature reasonably well.*

- **Homeowner Tip**: *Evaluate your exterior choices not just on looks but longevity. Spending a bit more on a 30-year roof vs a 15-year roof, or siding that needs less upkeep, can pay off in peace of mind and resale value. Also, consider adding **extra insulation** now if you can, even if not required by code, it's much cheaper to do in construction than retrofitting later. And if you live in a storm-prone area, think about impact-resistant windows or at least pre-install anchors for storm shutters now. Finally, as soon as that exterior is done, get a good lock on that new front door, your house is now dry and lockable, a big milestone for security and project momentum!*

Homeowner Summary, Exterior: Getting the exterior right is about balancing beauty and protection. The home's curb appeal comes from these finishes, but more importantly, they form the shell that keeps you safe from rain, wind, heat, and cold. Key takeaways: **water is the enemy**, guide it away at every opportunity (roof, walls, foundation), and **choose materials wisely** for your climate and maintenance tolerance. A well-built exterior means your home is low-maintenance and durable. You can then enjoy the fun part, picking paint colors, trim styles, and seeing your house's personality emerge, without worrying about leaks or premature repairs.

Chapter 5: Interior Rough-ins
Plumbing, Electrical, and HVAC

With the exterior shell completed, work moves inside. Before walls can be insulated and covered, the "rough-in" stage takes place for all the internal systems: **plumbing, electrical, and HVAC (Heating, Ventilation, and Air Conditioning)**. This is where the house truly becomes functional, getting its arteries and nerves. In this chapter, we break down each of these critical trades, explaining what's happening, what decisions are made, and how to ensure everything is done safely and up to code. Coordinating these systems is a big part of project management, there's an art to making sure pipes, wires, and ducts all coexist in the confines of your walls and ceilings without conflicts. We'll also highlight checkpoints and tests performed to verify these systems before closing up the walls.

5.1 Plumbing: Water In, Water Out

A home's plumbing is divided into two subsystems: the **water supply** (bringing in clean water under pressure to fixtures) and the **drain-waste-vent (DWV)** system (carrying used water and sewage out by gravity, and allowing air in so drains flow freely).

Water Supply Lines: In modern homes, these are typically either **copper pipes** or **PEX (cross-linked polyethylene) tubing**. Copper has been common for decades, it's durable and antimicrobial, but can be pricey and requires soldering joints (or newer press-fit connectors). PEX is a flexible plastic tubing that has become very popular due to lower cost and ease of installation (fewer fittings, as it can bend, and quick connections). Both can last a long time if installed properly. The main lines usually run from the water source (city meter or well) into a main shutoff, then branch to a water heater and to cold and hot lines for each fixture (sinks, toilets, showers, etc.). Plumbers often plan these runs to minimize turns and avoid conflicts with framing, drilling holes through studs or running lines through open web floor trusses. Insulating hot water lines is recommended (and sometimes code-mandated) to save energy and for quicker hot water to far fixtures.

Drain-Waste-Vent (DWV): This uses larger diameter pipes (usually PVC or ABS plastic piping nowadays) to remove wastewater via gravity. Every sink, toilet, tub, etc., has a drain that connects to branch lines, which connect to a **main stack** (often a vertical pipe going through the house) that then leads out to the sewer or septic. The vent part is crucial: those same pipes extend up through the roof (yes, those pipes you see sticking out above your roof are plumbing vents). They allow air into the system so that fixtures drain without creating suction that could siphon traps. **Traps** are the U-shaped sections under sinks or in toilets that hold water to block sewer gases from coming into the house. Every fixture must be trapped and vented properly per code.Plumbers during rough-in will install all these pipes, but none of the final fixtures yet (so you'll see pipe stubs sticking out where sinks, etc., will go). They'll also install **bathtub/shower units** or pans at this stage, because those often need to be set before walls are closed (many one-piece fiberglass tubs won't fit through finished doorways, so they go in while framing is open). They'll also run gas lines if the house has natural gas for a furnace, stove, etc. Gas lines can be black iron pipe or newer CSST flex tubing (yellow coated).

Plumbing Rough-In Inspection: The plumbing system (especially DWV) will typically be tested for leaks at rough-in. Often this is done by a **pressure or water test**: the drain system is filled with water to see if any joints leak, or pressurized with air. Supply lines might also be pressured up (say to 100 psi) and checked that they hold pressure. Inspectors ensure pipes have proper slope (generally 1/4 inch per foot for horizontal drains), that vent pipe sizing and distances meet code (for example, how far a trap can be from a vent stack without separate venting), and that appropriate materials and support are used.

- **Checklist:** *Plumbing Rough, All fixture locations confirmed (you don't want to discover later that a sink is off-center because a stud was in the way, adjust now if needed); drill holes in studs are within allowed diameter (not too large, and if they are near edges, protect with nail plates so screws later don't puncture pipes); water lines run with minimal bends, securely fastened (use pipe hangers, avoid them rattling); hot and cold lines correctly placed (hot on left, cold on right for fixtures); adequate clearance around toilet flange (usually need ~15" from center to wall); shower/tub valves at correct height; hose bibs (exterior faucets) installed with slight downward pitch to outside for drainage; main water shutoff* *accessible; pressure tests done (monitor gauges for any drop indicating leak); DWV slopes and vent tie-ins per plan (no illegal fittings like a horizontal tee where a wye is needed, etc.); trap arms within distance to vent as code; firestop any penetrations if required (some codes need special sealant where pipes go between floors for fire rating).*

- **Homeowner Tip:** *Take pictures of all plumbing runs before the walls are closed. You'll thank yourself if you ever need to locate a pipe to repair or avoid nailing into it. Also, discuss any special plumbing features now: do you want an outdoor gas line stub for a BBQ? An extra hose faucet on the side of the house? A future sink in the garage? It's easier to stub these in now than retrofit later. The same goes for a "rough-in" for a future bathroom in an unfinished basement, planning for that now by putting in drain stubs will save a lot of money if you add it down the road.*

5.2 Electrical: Wiring the Home

Your electrical system is like the nervous system of the house, carrying power to where it's needed for lights, appliances, and devices. It must be done with great care for safety (to prevent shocks and fires) and convenience (having enough outlets and lighting in the right spots).

Electrical Rough-in involves running cables (usually NM-B "Romex" cable in wood frame residential construction, which is a sheathed bundle of conductors) from the main electrical **panel** to all the switches, outlets, lights, and hardwired devices. The electrician will drill holes through studs and joists to snake these cables through, or run them along sides of framing (stapled neatly). They install electrical **boxes** (blue or metal boxes) at each outlet, switch, and fixture location. These boxes are set at standard heights (e.g., outlets ~12-16" above floor, switches ~48", but there's some variation by region or preference).

Circuits: The electrician divides the wiring into circuits, each protected by a breaker in the panel. For instance, kitchen outlets might be on two 20-amp circuits (modern codes require at least two "small appliance branch circuits" for kitchens), lighting might be on several 15-amp circuits, the microwave likely has its own, the furnace has its own, etc. Heavy appliances like oven, electric dryer, HVAC, will have dedicated higher-voltage circuits (240V circuits). Code also dictates things like bathrooms have a dedicated 20A circuit (or one that only serves multiple bathrooms), outdoor receptacles and garage on GFCI circuits, etc.

Safety Devices: Modern codes require **GFCI** (Ground Fault Circuit Interrupter) protection on outlets near water (kitchen counters, bathrooms, exterior, garages) and **AFCI** (Arc Fault Circuit Interrupter) protection on many circuits (bedrooms, living areas) to prevent fires from arcing faults. These can be breakers in the panel or special outlets. The electrician will wire accordingly. Smoke detectors (and CO detectors) are also wired at this stage, nowadays they must be interconnected (if one alarms, they all sound) and have battery backup, usually wired into a lighting circuit (so you notice if breaker is off).

 Low Voltage & Others: Also considered in rough electrical is running any low-voltage wiring like Ethernet/network cables, coax TV cables, speaker wires, alarm system wires, or smart home cabling. Often a different crew or the same electrician might handle these. It's wise to run extra conduits or cable for future tech needs while walls are open, if you desire (like CAT6 cables to each room for reliable internet, etc.).

Electrical Rough Inspection: The inspector will look for correct wire sizing (gauge matches breaker amperage), proper stapling and protection of cables (not too close to edge of studs unless metal plate used), fill of boxes (not too many wires jammed in a small box, volume matters to avoid overheating), that all connections are made in boxes (no hidden splices in walls), and that ground wires are properly connected. They also verify GFCI/AFCI plans, proper separation from plumbing (to avoid contact), and that holes in fire-rated areas (like top plates between floors) are sealed if required. The panel should be wired correctly with neutrals and grounds on proper bus bars, and breaker sizes appropriate. At rough-in, sometimes the panel isn't fully live yet (they might hook up to the grid later), but wiring should be complete.

- **Checklist**: *Electrical Rough, All outlet and switch boxes secured and at correct depth (flush with future drywall); correct number of receptacles in each room (generally every 12 feet of wall or 6 feet from any doorway/opening, per code, to avoid using extension cords); dedicated circuits for code-required appliances; kitchen and bath GFCIs planned; wires stripped and secured into boxes with enough slack (typically 6-8" of free conductor in each box); grounds all joined and pigtailed to metal boxes/devices; no damaged cables (watch out for nails piercing cable, those metal nail guard plates are needed wherever a cable is within 1.25" of stud face); light fixture boxes rated for fan if a fan is planned (they need special fan-rated boxes); keep low voltage separate from power cables (to avoid interference); coordinate exact locations for special things like under-cabinet lighting or wall ovens (the electrician might leave a coil of wire for appliance installers later); panel circuits labeled roughly (so inspector knows which is which).*

- **Homeowner Tip**: Walk through with your electrician if possible and think about everyday living: Are there enough outlets where you need them? (Consider places for charging devices, holiday lighting outlets under eaves, a floor outlet if you'll have lamps in middle of a room, etc.) It's much easier to add an outlet or move a light placement now than later. Also consider future needs: electric car charger in garage? Workshop tools? Home office equipment? Even if you don't install all now, maybe run conduit or cable for it. This is also the time to decide on lighting layout, where you want recessed lights, pendants, etc., and make sure the boxes are in the right spots. Lastly, take a video of the wiring before drywall, it can help locate a line if you ever need to cut into a wall or add something later without drilling into an existing cable (which is dangerous).

5.3 HVAC: Heating, Ventilation & Cooling

Your HVAC contractor (Heating, Ventilation, and Air Conditioning) will install the ducts, vents, and equipment that keep the house comfortable. This trade often overlaps with plumbing (for gas lines, flues) and electrical (for thermostats, furnace power) but has its own focus: moving air.

In a typical forced-air system (common in North America):

1. A **furnace** or heat pump with an air handler is installed (often in a basement, closet, or attic).
2. **Ductwork** (large trunks and smaller branch ducts) carries supply air to each room through **vents/registers**, and returns air from grills back to the unit.

3. For AC, an **outdoor condenser unit** is placed outside and connected via refrigerant lines to an **evaporator coil** in the furnace or air handler.
4. Ventilation may be integrated via bath fans, kitchen range hood, perhaps a fresh air intake or HRV/ERV (heat recovery ventilator) if the house is very tight.

During rough-in, the HVAC team will run big foil or fiberglass-insulated ducts or sometimes sheet metal ducts through joist spaces, walls, or attic to get air where it needs to go. They cut openings for supply registers (usually in floors for first floor if ducts in basement, or in ceilings if ducts in attic, or high on walls sometimes) and for return grills (often centrally located in hallways or multiple returns in larger homes). Placement is important: generally you supply air by windows or external walls to counteract drafts, and return air from central points.

They will also install exhaust ducts: every bathroom needs an exhaust fan ducted to outside; the kitchen will have a range hood vent (or at least a duct provision); the dryer vent is installed (4" metal duct to outside). These must be carefully routed with minimal bends and properly terminated outside with flappers or vent caps to prevent water/animals in.

HVAC Considerations: Sizing of equipment and ducts is done via Manual J and D calculations ideally (to ensure enough heating/cooling BTUs and proper airflow). Oversizing equipment is inefficient, under sizing fails to maintain comfort. Ducts need to be sized for the volume of air; too small ducts cause noise and insufficient air, too large and you lose velocity. All joints in ducts should be sealed (mastic or metal tape) to avoid leakage (leaky ducts waste energy, especially if running through attics or crawl spaces). Ducts in unconditioned spaces should be insulated to prevent condensation and energy loss.

If the home is multi-story, they might split into zones (two systems or dampers controlling different floors). Thermostat rough-in wires are run to a central location (often living area for main thermostat, maybe upstairs for second zone). Any gas furnace will need a vent (flue) pipe, typically a double-wall metal pipe up through the roof for combustion gases, unless it's a high-efficiency furnace which uses PVC pipes out the side wall (and draws its own combustion air through another PVC).

HVAC Rough Inspection: The inspector checks that ductwork is done according to code, which may include verifying proper support of ducts, fire blocking around ducts that penetrate fire-rated assemblies, correct materials (no flimsy flex duct where not allowed, no PVC on furnace flue unless condensing furnace, etc.), and that gas lines are tested (gas lines should be pressure tested by closing and seeing no drop over time). They also ensure dryer vent length isn't excessive or has too many bends (there are code limits because long dryer vents accumulate lint and can be fire hazard). Combustion venting clearance from combustibles, proper terminations of flues above roof, etc., are also checked.

- **Checklist:** HVAC Rough, *Main supply trunk and return installed, with branches to each room per plan; all ducts sealed at joints (use UL-181 rated tape or mastic, not common duct tape which fails over time); duct insulation in place for runs in attic or crawl; refrigerant line set run from indoor unit location to outside condenser location (ends capped to keep clean, and protected if running through framing); thermostat wire run to unit and to thermostat spot; bath fan boxes installed and ducted out (ensure a gentle slope to exterior or insulation around to avoid condensation pockets); range hood duct in place (typically 6" or larger smooth metal duct if a high CFM hood); dryer vent 4" duct with minimal elbows and route to an exterior wall with a good hood that has a damper;*

gas line pressure test (often ~15 psi air test on a gauge for 30 minutes, verify no drop); furnace or air handler set in place or at least platform ready (like a drip pan under units in attic in case of condensate overflow); condensate drain lines from AC coil roughed to an appropriate drain or exterior (and secondary pan drain if required); clearances maintained around furnace (e.g., some need a certain distance from walls).

- **Homeowner Tip:** *Think about comfort and furniture placement: if you like to put your couch against a certain wall, don't let a floor register end up right there blowing under it. Discuss any preferences with the HVAC installer, moving a vent a little now is easy. Also consider future finishing of spaces: if the basement is unfinished but you plan to finish later, have them stub ducts and returns in now for that area. Ask about fresh air options, modern homes benefit from controlled ventilation (some systems have an outside air intake or an ERV). Plan where the thermostat goes (typically an interior wall, five feet off floor, away from direct sun or drafts). If you have any special needs like a server closet that needs cooling or a sunroom that might need extra airflow, address it now. Lastly, have the HVAC installer show you the filter location and maintenance points on the furnace/air handler so you know how to change filters and where the shutoff switches are.*

5.4 Systems Coordination and the "MEP" Walkthrough

The term **MEP** stands for Mechanical, Electrical, Plumbing, the three main trades we've discussed. They often have to work in the same spaces. A famous coordination issue: who gets priority in a wall bay, the pipe, the duct, or the conduit? Good communication between trades (or a general contractor orchestrating them) is crucial so that, for example, an electrician doesn't cut a joist to run a cable where the plumber needed to put a big hole for a drain. Typically, the larger the object, the earlier it should be placed: plumbing drains are big and not flexible, so they go first; ducts next as they need space; wires last as they can weave around.

Before closing up, it's wise to do a **walkthrough with all trades or the GC** to double-check that nothing got missed. Are there any extra wires hanging that don't go anywhere? Any pipes without end caps? Does every light fixture opening have a wire? Is every plumbing fixture accounted for with a stub-out? Are all fireblocking foam/caulk done where mechanical penetrations go through top plates or floors (to maintain fire separation between levels, codes require sealing holes around pipes/wires)? This is the time to catch any oversight.

Then comes **MEP Inspection** (often the inspector does one combined inspection for all these at rough stage). Once that's passed, the project moves to insulating and closing walls (drywall).

- **Checklist**: *Pre-Close Inspection, All MEP rough inspections passed; any changes requested by inspector fixed (e.g., strap a pipe, add a nail guard plate, staple a wire, support a duct); walls cleared of debris; insulation baffles in place; sound insulation or special insulation (around bathrooms, bedrooms?) done if planned; take one more set of photos of everything in walls and ceilings; ensure all exterior penetrations are sealed (around pipes, wires, use caulk or foam); test the HVAC if possible (sometimes they will run the blower to test ducts, but often system isn't started until later to avoid construction dust in it); verify water lines hold pressure and drains are still clear (construction debris can find its way into an* *open drain, a rag left in a pipe accidentally, run a funnel of water through tub/shower drains to ensure they're open). After this, you're ready for insulation and drywall.*

- **Homeowner Tip**: *It might be a while before final fixtures go in, but start thinking about appliance and fixture selections now if you haven't. Some things like a heavy chandelier need blocking in attic or a fan rated box, which is best done now. If you're putting in anything like a wall oven or built-in microwave that has special electrical needs, confirm the electrician allowed for that circuit. Check that your washer water hookups and dryer duct are in a convenient spot (and your washer will fit in the allocated space). It's cheaper to tweak rough-in now than to rig extensions or whatnot later. Also, consider taking a video tour narrating what's inside the walls for your records, "here is the living room, that's a plumbing vent going up that corner, wires for outlets there..." It could be gold when troubleshooting something years later.*

Homeowner Summary, Rough-in Stage: The guts of your house, plumbing, wiring, and ductwork, may not be visible when you're living there, but they are vital to your comfort and safety. Quality here means leak-free plumbing, enough power and outlets for everything without tripping breakers, and even, quiet heating/cooling in all rooms. The rough-in is like the behind-the-scenes work that makes the magic happen when you flick a switch or turn a tap. For a smooth project, ensure good planning and communication among trades, and don't rush to cover things up until you're confident everything is correct. It's much easier to move a pipe or add an outlet now than after drywall. Embrace this not-so-pretty phase because it sets the stage for all the pretty finishes to function flawlessly. In the next chapter, we'll cover insulating and finishing those walls up!

Chapter 6: Insulation & Energy Efficiency

Now that the walls and ceilings are laced with the necessary infrastructure, it's time to wrap the home in a cozy blanket of **insulation** and take measures to ensure it remains energy-efficient and comfortable year-round. In this chapter, we delve into the materials and techniques that keep homes warm in winter, cool in summer, and generally efficient in their energy use. We also cover the important concepts of air sealing and ventilation, which go hand-in-hand with insulation in creating a healthy, efficient living environment. Given the growing emphasis on sustainability, this chapter will also highlight energy-efficient building techniques (some of which might overlap with our dedicated sustainable building chapter but we'll cover the basics here for completeness).

6.1 Thermal Insulation: Materials and R-Values

Insulation is what slows down heat transfer through the walls, roof, and floors of your home. It's measured by **R-value**, higher R means better insulating ability. Different materials achieve this in different ways (mostly by trapping air, since still air is a good insulator).

Common insulation types for residential construction:

1. **Fiberglass Batts:** These are fluffy blankets of spun glass fibers, often with a paper or foil facing (which can act as a vapor retarder). They are pre-cut to fit between standard stud or joist spacing (15" or 23" for 16" or 24" on-center framing). They're inexpensive and DIY-friendly, but to perform well, they must be installed carefully (no gaps, fluffing, or compression). A poorly installed R-19 batt full of gaps might perform like R-11 in reality.

2. **Blown-in Fiberglass or Cellulose:** These loose-fill insulations are blown into cavities using a machine. **Cellulose** is recycled newspaper treated for fire-resistance, which makes it quite eco-friendly. Both blown fiberglass and cellulose can fill gaps better than batts, especially if using a netted blown-in or dense-pack technique in walls. In attics, loose-fill is very common because it's easy to blow to the desired thickness (say, 12-20 inches, depending on climate).

3. **Spray Foam:** Comes in two types, **open-cell** (soft, expands a lot, slightly lower R per inch ~R-3.5) and **closed-cell** (rigid, higher R ~R-6 per inch, also acts as vapor barrier). Spray foam is pricy but it air-seals as it insulates. Closed-cell foam is often used in areas where you need a lot of R in a small space or need moisture barrier (like shallow roof rafters, or basement walls). It's great for high performance homes but cost can be 2-3x other methods.

4. **Rigid Foam Boards:** Typically used on exterior of walls (continuous insulation) or in basements. Types include EPS (expanded polystyrene), XPS (extruded polystyrene, e.g., Styrofoam blue board), and Polyiso (polyisocyanurate). They offer R-4 to R-6 per inch. Foam boards can be cut and fitted between studs too, though laborious. They also are used to insulate slab edges or as radiant floor insulation etc.

5. **Mineral Wool (Rockwool):** These batts or boards are made from spun rock or slag. They are fireproof (unlike fiberglass, which can melt, rockwool can withstand very high temps) and water-resistant (don't soak up water like cellulose might). They have similar or slightly higher R than fiberglass and are a bit denser, which also gives some soundproofing advantage. They're also mold-resistant due to inorganic content.

6. **Reflective Insulations:** Foil-faced bubble wrap or radiant barriers can help in attics by reflecting radiant heat (especially beneficial in hot climates to keep attic heat

down). They are used as supplements, not usually standalone main insulation.

Where to Insulate: Per code and good practice:

- All exterior walls (including walls between house and an unheated garage), typically R-13 to R-21 depending on climate & construction.
- Attic/ceiling, usually highest R (R-38 to R-60 in colder zones).
- Floor over unheated spaces (like floor above crawlspace or cantilever), R-19 to R-30 often.
- Basement walls or crawlspace walls, if conditioned or to meet energy code, maybe R-10 to R-15 continuous or R-13 cavity, etc.
- Additionally, insulating interior walls or floors for **sound** is sometimes done for bathrooms, bedrooms (not required by code, but an upgrade for comfort/privacy).

Vapor Barriers/Retarders: In colder climates, one often installs a vapor retarder on the **warm-in-winter side** of the insulation (usually the interior, facing heated space) to prevent moist indoor air from diffusing into cold walls where it could condense. This could be a kraft paper on a batt, a poly sheet, or simply well-detailed paint (paint can act as a vapor retarder class III in some assemblies). In hot humid climates, it's tricky, often you don't want a vapor barrier on the inside, as the outside is humid; you might let the wall dry inward and instead have an exterior vapor retarder. The science of this can be complex; thankfully, modern codes and products specify what to use for typical conditions. The key is **avoid trapping moisture**, there should typically not be two impermeable layers sandwiching a wall.

Air Sealing: This goes along with insulation, tiny cracks can let a lot of air (and thus heat) leak. Before or during insulation, builders will caulk or spray foam gaps: e.g., where wires or pipes penetrate top and bottom plates, at exterior wall band joists, around window frames shims, etc. Many jurisdictions now require a blower door test to ensure the house is tight (but not too tight, hence ventilation is important). Air sealing is often the most cost-effective way to improve efficiency and comfort (no drafts).

- **Checklist**: *Insulation & Air Seal, All exterior wall penetrations (plumbing, wiring, vents) sealed with caulk or expandable foam; any big gaps around window/door frames foamed (low-expansion foam for windows to not warp frames); recessed light fixtures are IC-rated and sealed (or boxed in) if in insulated ceilings; baffle vents at eaves in attic to keep insulation from blocking ventilation; attic hatch insulated or weatherstripped; batts cut neatly around electrical boxes (no gaps, don't stuff a big batt behind pipes compressing it too much, either split the batt or use foam/loose-fill behind); no "thermal bypasses" left (for example, the wall between floors at a balloon framing cavity or open chases around plumbing, must be blocked and insulated so it's not a chimney of air loss); vapor barrier installed correctly where needed (no tears, overlaps sealed, not on wrong side); insulation depth in attic blown to required thickness (mark with rulers stapled to trusses indicating inches to verify R-value); insulation around windows/doors but not on top of electrical heat sources (don't cover a recessed can light that isn't rated for contact with insulation).*
- **Homeowner Tip**: *More insulation is generally better up to a point of diminishing returns. If you're in a cold climate and code says R-49 in attic, going to R-60 is relatively cheap and will further reduce heat loss. But upgrading walls from R-20 to R-30 might be harder (requires thicker walls or special*

techniques). During construction, if you feel some spots might be leaky or thin, speak up. Also consider sound insulation: adding rockwool batts inside bathroom walls or between floors can deaden sound significantly, relatively cheap during build, impossible later. If you plan to finish a basement eventually, insulate the rim joist and maybe the basement walls now, even if just with temporary fiber batts or foam board, to make it less chilly. Lastly, ask the builder for the results of any blower door test or insulation inspection, a tight house with proper ventilation (see next section) will be more comfortable and cheaper to run.

6.2 Ventilation and Indoor Air Quality

As we tighten up houses, we must ensure **fresh air** can get in when needed and stale or moist air can get out. Ventilation can be **natural** (air leaks, opening windows) or **mechanical** (fans, dedicated systems). Building codes now often require a *mechanical ventilation* strategy for new homes because they are built so tight that natural leakage isn't enough for healthy air exchange.

Key ventilation points:

i. **Spot Ventilation:** Bath fans and kitchen hoods we mentioned, these remove moisture and odors at the source. Always vent them directly outside (not into attic!). Use them as needed, e.g., run the bath fan during and 10 min after a shower.

ii. **Whole-House Ventilation:** Some homes use an **HRV/ERV** (Heat Recovery Ventilator / Energy Recovery Ventilator). These are dedicated systems that pull in fresh outside air and exhaust stale inside air, transferring heat (and in ERV, moisture) between the streams to save energy. They often tie into the HVAC ducts or have their own small duct network. If not an HRV/ERV, at minimum, some new homes might rely on an automatic timer that kicks on the HVAC fan with a damper that brings in outside air (mixing fresh air into the system). Or a simple exhaust fan that runs continuously at low speed and passive inlets in walls to let air in.

iii. **Attic Ventilation:** We must also ventilate the attic (if it's not a conditioned attic) to prevent moisture and heat buildup. Soffit vents + ridge vents are a common combo. Ensure insulation doesn't block soffit vents (hence baffles). In hot climates, radiant barriers or attic fans might be used too.

iv. **Crawl Space Ventilation vs. Encapsulation:** Traditional crawl spaces had vents to outside. But many newer practices lean towards conditioning or encapsulating crawl spaces (closing vents, insulating walls, and maybe dehumidifying) to avoid moisture issues. Whatever the strategy, it should be executed as designed, if encapsulated, make sure poly vapor barrier on ground is sealed, vents closed, perhaps a small duct from HVAC or a dehumidifier is in place.

v. **Combustion Ventilation:** If you have any fuel-burning appliances (gas furnace, water heater, wood stove), ensure proper venting of those (flues) and adequate combustion air supply if needed (some furnaces have dedicated intake from outside).

vi. **Indoor Air Quality (IAQ):** Besides fresh air, watch out for **off-gassing** materials (use low-VOC paints and finishes if possible), and consider a good filtration system on your HVAC (a decent MERV-rated filter or even HEPA if allergies are concern). Keep in mind that new builds often have construction dust, a thorough cleaning before moving in is wise.

- **Checklist**: *Ventilation, Ridge and soffit vents clear; any powered attic fan functioning (with thermostat if installed); bathroom fans ducted out (flapper on exterior present); range hood vent installed (and if it's a powerful hood, check if a makeup air inlet is required by code, some places require if hood > 400 CFM to prevent backdrafting of chimneys); verify function of HRV/ERV if present (test it, correct flow balancing by HVAC tech); set furnace blower fan to "auto" or "intermittent" per whatever ventilation strategy (some systems have controllers to run fan a set amount each hour to mix air); crawl space, if vented, are vents unobstructed? If encapsulated, is everything sealed and possibly a dehu or small vent in place?; ensure the clothes dryer vent opens freely (no blockage, no screen that can catch lint); all vent terminations have critter screens where appropriate (except dryer which shouldn't have a fine screen, just a flap); educate homeowner on how to operate any ventilation controls (some might have a boost switch for HRV or know to clean HRV filters).*

- **Homeowner Tip**: *Proper ventilation is key to avoiding that "stuffy" feeling or worse, mold problems. Don't underestimate the importance of bath fans, use them and consider ones with a humidistat or timer so they run automatically when needed. If you find condensation on windows in winter, that's a sign you need more ventilation (or less humidification). Consider getting a small meter that shows temperature and humidity; keeping indoor humidity around 30-50% is ideal (lower in winter to avoid window condensation, higher in summer for comfort but under 60% to prevent mold). And remember, if your house is very tight,* open the windows occasionally! *On a nice day, an hour of fresh breeze can do wonders. The investment in energy efficiency means you can afford to bring in fresh air without huge energy penalties, especially if heat recovery is in place. Balance efficiency with livability.*

6.3 Energy-Efficient Building Techniques

(This section provides a bridge to the dedicated sustainable building chapter to come, but introduces some techniques commonly employed.)

Beyond just insulation, there are several advanced techniques and technologies to make a home more energy-efficient:

- **Passive Solar Design:** Orienting the house and its windows to capitalize on the sun's heat in winter and block it in summer. This might mean lots of south-facing glass with overhangs that shade in high summer sun, and perhaps thermal mass (like a concrete floor) that absorbs heat and releases it slowly.
- **High-Efficiency Windows:** Windows are the weakest link in insulation (even good ones are maybe R-3 to R-5). Using double or triple-pane windows with Low-E coatings and argon fill can dramatically improve performance. For example, triple-pane windows in cold climates keep heat in much better and also nearly eliminate condensation and cold drafts near windows.
- **Advanced Framing (Optimum Value Engineering):** Techniques like 2x6 studs at 24" on center (instead of 2x4 @ 16), aligning studs with trusses to eliminate double top plate, using single studs at corners or insulated headers, etc., can reduce thermal bridging (less wood, more insulation in the wall). Less wood also means less resource use. It has to be balanced with structural needs, but it's in the code as options.
- **Continuous Insulation and Thermal Breaks:** As mentioned, putting foam board outside the sheathing or using insulated siding can greatly boost wall R-value by preventing heat from leaking through the wood studs (wood is about R-1 per inch, not much). Even using spray

foam in walls vs batts can improve airtightness and performance. Insulating the foundation exterior, slab edges, etc., also can be done.

- **Cool Roofs and Green Roofs:** In hot climates, using roofing materials that reflect more sun (high Solar Reflective Index, SRI) can keep the home cooler and reduce AC loads. Green roofs (vegetation layer) add insulation and reduce heat gain too, though usually more on specialized builds.

- **Efficient HVAC and Water Heating:** A high-efficiency furnace (e.g., 95% AFUE vs an older 80%) or better yet a **heat pump** (which can provide heating and cooling efficiently) will cut energy bills. Heat pumps now work in fairly cold climates efficiently. On water heaters, tankless or heat pump water heaters use less energy than old resistive tanks.

- **Solar Panels:** More homes now include photovoltaic (PV) solar panels on the roof to generate electricity. While not a part of construction per se, roof design can include conduit runs for future solar, and an electrical panel that can handle the connection. Some codes (like California) even mandate solar on new homes.

- **Smart Home Systems:** Using smart thermostats and controls can optimize energy use (e.g., learning your schedule to lower heat when you're away, etc.). Lighting with all LED bulbs reduces electricity usage significantly and produces less heat, easing AC load as well.

- **Energy Star / Certifications:** Building to programs like ENERGY STAR Homes, LEED, or Passive House provides frameworks for efficiency. For instance, a Passive House design aims for such low energy use that a small mini-split can heat the whole house. These often require very high insulation, airtightness (0.6 ACH @50Pa or better), HRV ventilation, and minimal thermal bridging.

To tie this back to the homeowner perspective: these techniques might mean a slightly higher build cost (insulation upgrades, better windows can add cost) but result in **20-30% (or more) energy savings** and a more comfortable home with fewer drafts and temperature swings. Many people find that worth the investment, especially as energy prices rise. We will explore more of this in the sustainable building chapter, but for now, your home at this stage should meet at least the baseline energy code.

Performing a **blower door test** and **thermal imaging scan** before drywall or right after insulation can catch any leaks or gaps. Some builders do a blower door while a house is under construction to find and fix leaks (called an AeroBarrier process or just a manual find-and-seal).

- *Checklist. Energy Efficiency QA*, Insulation meets or exceeds code R-values everywhere; no obvious gaps (e.g., behind tubs on exterior walls, often a missed spot, ensure it's insulated before tub install, or the band joist areas); all penetrations sealed; duct insulation on any ducts outside conditioned space; high-efficiency windows and doors installed with proper sealing; HVAC equipment size and efficiency ratings documented; if getting a HERS rating (Home Energy Rating Score), schedule rater visit for testing; verify thermostat is programmable or smart; water heater insulation blanket added (if standard tank type); check for any rebates or incentives, at this point many utilities or governments will offer rebates for things like better HVAC, insulation, or solar, make sure paperwork is in line.
- *Homeowner Tip:* A super-insulated house can **save you tens of thousands of dollars** over its life in utility bills, and it feels more comfortable. It's one of those things that's hidden in the walls, but you'll notice every month in what you *don't* pay for heating/cooling. If you can, put

a bit extra into insulation or better windows now, it's generally worth it. Also, keep in mind your home is a system: sealing it tightly means you must use ventilation correctly (as mentioned). Once you move in, keep an eye on your energy usage and comfort, if something seems off (like one room always hotter), bring it up with the builder because it might be an airflow balance issue or missed insulation. Finally, enjoy the benefits: fewer drafts, quieter indoors (insulation also blocks noise), and pride that you've built a home that's kind to both your wallet and the planet.

Homeowner Summary, Insulation & Efficiency: This phase might not be visually exciting (you see a lot of fluffy stuff and foam), but it is arguably one of the most important for the long-term performance of your home. A well-insulated, well-sealed house will be **cheaper to heat and cool, more comfortable to live in, and have a smaller environmental footprint**. Attention to detail here is critical: one uninsulated corner or a leaky attic hatch can undermine otherwise great work. So, builders must take care, and homeowners should be aware of what's going into their walls and attics. In short, *don't skimp on insulation*. It's the gift that keeps on giving, every winter and summer for the life of the home. With this done, we're ready to move to the finishes that you will see and touch every day, the interior finishes and fixtures.

Chapter 7: Interior Finishes
From Drywall to Decor

With the technical heavy-lifting of structure, systems, and insulation complete, the focus shifts to making the interior of the house livable and beautiful. **Interior finishes** encompass a broad range of tasks and materials: drywall installation, interior trim (like crown molding and baseboards), doors, cabinets, painting, flooring, and all the aesthetic touches. This is the stage where the space transforms from a shell with exposed studs to actual rooms. It's often one of the longer phases because of the level of detail and the number of trades involved (drywall finishers, trim carpenters, painters, tile setters, etc.). In this chapter, we'll outline the key steps of interior finishing, provide tips for quality and durability, and give checklists to ensure nothing is missed. We'll also touch on the final **inspections** and preparations leading to moving in.

7.1 Drywall (Sheetrock) Installation and Finishing

Drywall, also known as Sheetrock (a brand name) or wallboard, is the common material for interior walls and ceilings. These gypsum boards (usually 4×8, 4×12, or even larger sheets) are screwed to the framing, then finished with joint compound to create a smooth (or textured) continuous surface ready for paint.

Hanging Drywall: Typically done by a crew that moves quickly, they'll use lifts or just brute force to hang ceiling boards first (usually 1/2" thick on ceilings, sometimes 5/8" for fire code or extra stiffness, or even special sag-resistant board). Then walls are hung, with boards oriented either horizontally (most common) or vertically depending on ceiling height and preference. They cut out openings for electrical boxes, can lights, etc., usually with rotozip tools or saws. Key is to hit the studs with the screws (there are screw guns set to proper depth so the screw head dimples the paper just right without breaking through too much). Gaps between sheets should be minimized but a small gap is okay (will be filled). Drywall comes in moisture-resistant varieties (green board, purple board) for use in bathrooms or behind tile, and cement board is used behind showers or tile areas that will get wet.

Taping and Mudding: After hanging, tapers come in. They apply joint tape (either paper tape or self-adhesive mesh) over all seams and embed it in a first coat of joint compound ("mud"). They also cover screw dimples with a first coat. Inside corners get paper tape folded and mudded; outside corners get metal or plastic corner bead applied for crisp edges, then mudded over. This first coat is often called a "tape coat." Then they let it dry (usually overnight or more, unless using fast setting compound).

Next, a **second coat** of mud goes on, wider, to cover and feather out the seams. This dries. Then a **third coat** (finish coat) with an even wider knife (maybe 10-12 inches wide) to feather it further, making the joint invisible. After all coats are done and dry, they **sand** the dried compound to smooth it (a potentially dusty job, good crews will use pole sanders and maybe vacuums, and wear masks).

Sometimes a **texture** is applied instead of leaving walls smooth (depending on regional style or to hide minor imperfections). Common textures: "orange peel" (fine splatter), "knock-down" (splatter then troweled slightly), or "popcorn" (rarely used now, mainly older ceilings).

Quality considerations: Good finishers can make seams disappear. Level 4 finish (standard) is usually fine for walls that will be painted with flat paint. For gloss paint or critical lighting walls (light casting shallow angle), a Level 5 finish (an extra skim coat over everything) is recommended to avoid seeing any imperfections. In bathrooms or where tiles go, less finishing is needed on areas to be tiled (just taped is fine under tile).

- *Checklist: Drywall, Correct type of drywall in correct areas (moisture-resistant in baths, fire-rated where required like garages/house wall, or ceilings under living space in basements if needed; cement board in shower wet walls); all seams properly taped (no loose tape); sufficient screws (generally 8" apart on edges, 12" on field for ceilings, etc.); no screws popping or not properly dimpled; corners straight and smooth, surfaces sanded with no ridges or pocks (shine a light along the wall to check); minimal dust left (the crew should at least broom sweep, though fine dust may remain, vacuum before painting); any removed or covered vent openings, etc. cleared (sometimes mud or debris can fall in ducts or cover an outlet, check all outlets and fixtures are accessible).*

- **Homeowner Tip:** *Walk around after primer (usually the drywall crew or painters will prime the walls). Primer makes any remaining imperfections more visible. If you see obvious dents, ridges, or uneven corners, point them out to be fixed before final paint. This is also the time to decide if you want any special wall textures or finishes. Also, consider that after drywall, the house is pretty closed up, now is a good time to bring in any large furniture or items that might not fit later (though usually doorways are big enough). Drywall is also the stage where it really looks like a house inside, enjoy it! It might also echo a lot (bare walls/floors), that will change us finishes like flooring and curtains come in.*

7.2 Interior Millwork: Doors, Trim, and Built-Ins

Once the walls are done (and often even painted with a first coat), carpenters come in to install **interior doors, trim, and millwork**. This is the fine carpentry part that adds character and polish.

Interior Doors: These can be pre-hung units (a door already hinged to a jamb) or slab doors hung on site. Pre-hung is common: the carpenter shims the jamb in the rough opening, making it plumb and level so the door swings correctly, then nails the jamb to the studs through the shims, and trims out. Doors can be hollow-core (cheaper, lighter, used for most rooms) or solid-core (better soundproofing, higher quality feel, often used for entry to master bedroom or as specified). Don't forget closet doors (bifold, sliding, etc., each installed as per their type), and any pocket doors (those would have been roughed-in with a special frame earlier, now get the actual door slab installed on the track).

Trim (Molding): This includes:

i.   **Baseboards:** Trim along the bottom of walls at the floor. These cover the drywall edge and give a finished look. They can be simple or ornate. They're usually nailed to the wall bottom plate/studs.
ii. **Casing:** Trim around doors and windows. They hide the gap between the door frame and wall and add style. Miters at the corners should be tight.
iii. **Crown Molding:** Decorative trim at the ceiling-wall junction in some rooms for an elegant touch.
iv. **Other Trim:** Chair rails, wainscoting panels, mantelpieces, built-in shelves or benches, window sills or aprons, etc., depending on design.

v. **Stair parts:** If the house has stairs, trim carpenters also install railings, balusters, newel posts, and trim on skirt boards, etc. Stairs are both structural and finish, hopefully the rough stairs were set earlier and now the finishes like treads, risers, and railings go on.

Cabinetry and Built-ins: Often towards the end of trim stage or just after, kitchen cabinets, bathroom vanities, and any built-in cabinets (like a mudroom cubby or bookshelves) are installed. These are usually pre-made and just secured to walls (ensuring they're level and plumb). It's critical for countertops that base cabinets are level and in one plane.

Attention to Detail: Trim work may seem just cosmetic, but it requires precision. Misaligned trim can look bad and catch the eye. Carpenters will fill nail holes and caulk edges (especially between trim and wall) to prepare for painting. If doing stained (not painted) wood trim, that's a higher bar because caulk can't hide joints, everything must fit very tightly, and nail holes must be filled with color-matched putty.

- **Checklist**: Millwork, *All doors open and close smoothly without rubbing (check clearance at top/bottom, especially if flooring not in yet, they may need to cut bottoms later to fit over carpet); door latches line up with strike plates; no split jambs or trim, if a piece split on nailing, it should be replaced; consistent reveal (gap) around doors between jamb and door and between casing and jamb; trim joints (miters, scarf joints in long runs) tight and/or properly filled; baseboards level on top and tight to floor (some gaps might be covered by quarter-round shoe molding after flooring if floors are uneven); railing is solid (no wobble in stair parts, balusters spaced per code, usually <4" gap); cabinets are securely anchored (give a little tug, they shouldn't move* *or creak); drawers and doors align nicely; any custom built-ins are as per design and securely fixed; everything is ready for paint/touch-ups (holes filled, etc.).*

- **Homeowner Tip**: *Before painting is the time to decide on any changes like adding extra trim or different styles (it's harder once painted). If you want to add something like wall paneling or decorative beams, talk now. Also, as soon as trim is done is often when the house is measured for countertops, if stone, and when you might want to start thinking about hardware (door knobs, cabinet pulls) and closet organizers. Ensure you like how door swings are (some people realize a door would be better swinging opposite, a pain to change later but doable now if need be). Check sightlines: does any door swing block a light switch? Sometimes small adjustments save annoyance (like swapping a door to swing out of a small bathroom instead of in, if code allows and it's safe). It's much easier to change a door swing or widen a casing now than after paint.*

7.3 Painting and Decorating

With trim in and everything caulked and prepped, it's time for **painting**, which dramatically changes the feel of the house. Painters will:

i. Apply a primer coat (if not already done after drywall).

ii. Then two finish coats on walls (usually flat, matte, or eggshell for living spaces; maybe satin or semi-gloss in kitchens/baths for washability), and on the ceiling (often flat white).

iii. Trim is typically painted separately (often semi-gloss or gloss white or the chosen trim color). If wood stain is used on trim or doors, that's a different process (stain and clear polyurethane coats).

iv. They'll also paint exterior door(s) now if not already finished, and any other paintable items like built-ins, or perhaps the garage interior, etc.

Color selection is a big homeowner decision but from a building viewpoint, once chosen, the painters should neatly cut in lines, no drips, etc. Good painters mask off and cover floors/cabinets, remove or carefully tape hardware, etc.

Also at this stage, **wallpapering or special finishes** would be done after painting (for accent walls maybe). Tiling of backsplashes or tub surrounds might also happen around now if not earlier (tile usually after drywall but before final paint, since it can be messy).

- **Checklist**: *Paint & Finishes, Even coverage (no patchiness or showing through) on all painted surfaces; clean cut lines between trim and wall colors (or ceiling and wall); no paint on fixtures, floors, or windows (small speckles can be scraped off glass, but should be minimal); correct color and sheen as per spec; touch-up paint left behind for homeowner (usually they give you labeled cans for each color for future fixes); if any staining, check for consistency and no blotches; all protective tapes removed and trash cleared.*

- **Homeowner Tip**: *Walk through and note any areas for paint touch-up (most builders have this on their punch list). Check corners and edges. Look at walls in both daylight and artificial light, sometimes you'll spot a missed second coat area. Minor imperfections can be fixed easily now. Also, consider where you might want wall decor and maybe ask for blocking if heavy items, although by now walls are closed, but you can still use special anchors. This is also the time to finalize where bathroom accessories (towel bars, TP holder, etc.) go, sometimes the trim carpenter or hardware installer will put them in, or you do after move-in, but think about heights and positions now (there may be blocking in the wall from earlier for this if planned).*

7.4 Flooring Installation

Flooring usually goes in after paint (so you're not dripping paint on new floors) but before final trim shoe moldings and before final plumbing fixtures (to set toilets on top of finished floor, etc.). Types of flooring include:

1. **Hardwood (or engineered wood):** Either nailed down (for solid wood) or glued/floated for engineered. Wood needs acclimation in the house for a few days prior. After install, if site-finished, it gets sanded and clear coated (that can be a fume-heavy and dust-generating job, often near the end). Prefinished wood is already coated, just install and done.

2. **Tile:** Ceramic or porcelain tile, common for bathrooms, kitchens, entries. Tile is set with mortar on a substrate (cement board or special membrane over subfloor) and then grouted. It's a slower process. Make sure it's well planned (pattern, no small slivers at edges, properly spaced).

3. **Carpet:** Usually last, as it's quickest. Padding laid, then carpet stretched in or glued (commercial). Seams should be invisible, and the direction consistent unless intentionally patterned.

4. **Laminate or Vinyl Plank:** These click-together floating floors or glue-down vinyl are common as economical choices. They go in easily and often last.

5. **Concrete (stained/polished):** If the design calls for exposed concrete floors (modern style or basement), that would have been decided early and the slab protected. Finishing of that might happen now (like polishing or sealing).

Flooring transitions between materials need coordination, e.g., a marble threshold at a bathroom, or a T-molding between wood and tile if needed. Also, floor installers should undercut jambs so flooring slides underneath for a clean look, and install base shoe molding after to cover expansion gaps.

- **Checklist**: *Flooring, Subfloor was clean, level, and appropriate underlayment used (for tile, cement board or Ditra, etc., for wood maybe rosin paper, for vinyl maybe lauan plywood underlayment if needed, etc.); no squeaks (if any subfloor squeaks left, they should fix by screwing before covering with floor); flooring material installed with correct expansion gaps at edges for wood/laminate; no hollow sounds or loose tiles (tap tiles for proper adhesion); grout lines consistent and full (no gaps or excessively uneven lines); wood floors straight and tight (no large gaps, end joints staggered nicely); carpet stretched tight (no wrinkles or loose spots) and edges tucked neatly; transitions pieces secure and even; floor is clean and protected (often they may cover it with paper or plastic to prevent damage from remaining work).*

- **Homeowner Tip**: *Ask for leftover flooring pieces or a box of tiles to keep in storage, if you ever need a repair, matching from the same dye lot helps. For hardwood, know the brand/color for future additions. Also, note the maintenance: when can you move furniture onto new wood finish? (Usually after 24-48 hours if finished in place). Avoid washing tiles until grout fully cures (per installer advice). Also, consider door clearances: often after thick carpet install, some doors might rub, the carpenters should trim door bottoms beforehand if needed, check this. Lastly, flooring can be a personal design element, ensure it meets your expectations now, because changing it later is disruptive and costly.*

7.5 Fixtures and Final Touches

We're nearing completion. Now all the parts that were roughed in get their final fixtures:

a. **Plumbing Fixtures:** Toilets, sinks, faucets, showerheads, etc., are installed. Water supply connections (with shutoff valves) and drain hookups are made. Caulk is applied around edges of fixtures (like around tub to wall joint, sink to counter, etc.). Water heater is fired up if not already. The plumber will test for leaks in these connections.

b. **Electrical Fixtures:** Light fixtures and fans are hung, outlets and switches get their cover plates, smoke detectors installed, the electrical panel gets any final breakers labeled clearly. Doorbells, thermostats, and any other low-voltage stuff (alarm keypads, etc.) installed. At this point, all electrical should be "live" and tested, lights turning on, outlets tested with a tester (for correct wiring and GFCI function).

c. **HVAC Final:** Thermostats installed, furnace started, AC charged with refrigerant and tested (if summer, or at least verified charge). Registers adjusted for airflow, and any last pieces like installing return air grills. Gas furnace or water heater venting double-checked for proper draft.

d. **Hardware and Accessories:** All door knobs and locks installed and working (and keys provided). Cabinet knobs/pulls attached. Bathroom accessories (towel bars, mirrors, shower rods, toilet paper holders) put up. Closet rods and shelves installed (or closet organizer systems put in).

e. **Glass and Shower Doors:** If you have custom shower glass enclosures, those are measured after tile and installed now. Mirrors in bathrooms put up (unless using separate mirrors).

f. **Painting Touch-ups:** With everything in place, painters often come for a last touch-up round to fix any scuffs or fill any nail holes from hardware installs.

g. **Cleaning:** A thorough cleaning of all surfaces, removing dust, stickers on windows, excess paint drops, etc. Often a professional cleaning crew will do a "builder's clean."

At the end of all this, the house should be essentially complete.

- **Checklist**: Final Fixtures, *All plumbing fixtures tight (no drips under sinks, open cabinets and feel for leaks after running water; toilets secure and not rocking on floor; hot water comes out of correct side of faucets; good water pressure and proper drainage without gurgling); water heater set to appropriate temperature (~120°F to avoid scalding but still hot enough); furnace/AC running, check air coming out vents and return suction; electrical: every switch and outlet tested (bring a small device or tester, especially test GFCI outlets and AFCI breakers via test buttons); all lights work (no bulbs out, unless they expect you to supply your own bulbs in fixtures); smoke/CO alarms chirp on test; insulation in attic is not disturbed (some workers may push aside insulation to install a light and forget to put it back, peek in attic if easily accessed to ensure uniform coverage); doors latch properly with trim on (sometimes after painting, alignment can shift slightly, adjust strikes if needed); windows fully cleaned and moving freely (no paint stuck, locks working, screens in place); check any special features (e.g., irrigation system, if installed, or central vacuum if that's a thing, etc.); verify all keys (multiple copies for each lock) and garage door openers are given; exterior grading final check (water should drain away from house); any remaining construction debris removed from yard.*

- **Homeowner Tip**: *This is your **walkthrough time**, also called punch list or new home orientation. Don't be shy* *about noting issues, even small ones like a caulk line missed or a cabinet door slightly misaligned. It's normal to have a list of a few dozen touch-ups in a new build. Check surfaces for scratches or damage (flooring, counters, tubs). Test all appliances (if they are included), run the dishwasher, turn on range burners briefly, etc. Also, now's a good time to learn: ask where the main water shutoff is, how to change HVAC filters, etc. Good builders will acquaint you with these. Understand warranty procedures for if something goes wrong in the first year (many have a 1-year general warranty). And finally, celebrate! You've gone from an idea to a fully constructed home.*

Homeowner Summary, Interior Finishing: This final phase is like the grand finale of a fireworks show, lots of activity, lots of transformation, and then a satisfying completion. By focusing on quality during finishes (from smooth drywall to tight-fitting trim and well-installed floors), builders create the comfort and beauty homeowners dream of. For homeowners, this stage tests patience because it's the last 10% that can feel like it takes 90% of the time, but the reward is seeing your vision materialize. Keep a careful eye on details, communicate any concerns, and soon you'll be placing furniture and enjoying your new home. Every paint color, tile pattern, and fixture finish comes together now, this is where your house truly becomes *your* home.

Chapter 8: Sustainable Building Techniques

(In this dedicated chapter, we expand on the concepts introduced earlier, focusing on building "green", methods and materials that reduce environmental impact and improve efficiency, often exceeding standard practice.)

Building sustainably isn't just a trendy choice, it's rapidly becoming an essential part of modern construction. Not only do energy-efficient, eco-friendly homes lower utility costs and increase comfort for homeowners, they also **reduce the carbon footprint** of our built environment and often prove more durable in the long run. This chapter covers sustainable and energy-efficient techniques in a comprehensive way: from design considerations to material choices and technology integrations. Whether you're aiming for a certified green building or simply want to incorporate a few green ideas, this chapter provides practical guidance.

8.1 The Principles of Sustainable Home Design

At its core, sustainable home design revolves around a few key principles:

i.   **Energy Efficiency:** Minimizing the energy required to heat, cool, and power the home. This includes the building envelope (insulation, windows), efficient systems (HVAC, lighting, appliances), and possibly on-site renewable energy production.

ii. **Water Efficiency:** Reducing water usage via efficient fixtures, smart irrigation, and capturing rainwater or reusing greywater if possible.

iii.   **Resource-efficient Materials:** Using materials that are recycled, have low environmental impact in production, or are high durability (so they don't need frequent replacement). Also, minimizing waste during construction.

iv.   **Healthy Indoor Environment:** Ensuring good indoor air quality with proper ventilation and using low-emission materials (low-VOC paints, formaldehyde-free cabinetry, etc.) so the home's indoor environment promotes health.

v.   **Site Impact:** Orienting and designing the home to work with the local climate and conditions (passive solar, preserving existing trees, preventing soil erosion during construction, etc.), and landscaping with native plants requiring minimal irrigation.

A well-known framework is the **LEED for Homes or National Green Building Standard**, which provide checklists and points for various green measures. Even without formal certification, following their guidelines can ensure you're hitting major sustainability targets.

8.2 Energy-Efficient Technologies and Strategies

We've covered insulation and air sealing thoroughly, which are fundamental. Let's look at additional technologies and strategies:

A. High-Performance HVAC: Traditional HVAC can be a big energy hog. Newer alternatives:

- **Heat Pumps:** These electric devices provide both heating and cooling by moving heat rather than generating it. Modern air-source heat pumps can work in cold climates efficiently. **Geothermal (ground-source) heatpumps** use steady ground temperatures to be even more efficient (but have high upfront cost due to buried loops).

- **Zoning:** Instead of one thermostat for the whole house, zoning systems allow different areas to be controlled separately, so you're not overheating empty rooms. This can be done with multiple small systems or a central system with motorized dampers.
- **Ductless Mini-splits:** These are heat pump units that don't require ductwork. Great for retrofit or for providing independent control to, say, an addition or a seldom-used guest room.
- **Energy Recovery Ventilators (ERVs) / Heat Recovery Ventilators (HRVs):** As mentioned, these provide fresh air with minimal energy penalty. In a truly tight house, these are key.
- **Smart Thermostats:** Learning thermostats or web-connected ones that optimize usage by learning patterns or using geofencing (detecting when you're away via phone) can save 10-15% on HVAC energy by eliminating wasteful heating/cooling.

B. Renewable Energy Integration:

- **Solar Photovoltaic (PV) Panels:** Prices have dropped dramatically, making rooftop solar viable in many areas. A properly sized solar array can offset a significant portion of the home's electric use, or even all of it in a net-zero energy home.
- **Solar Hot Water:** Solar thermal panels can preheat water, reducing water heater load.
- **Battery Storage:** Home batteries (like Tesla Powerwall or others) can store solar energy for use at night or during outages. Not common in all homes yet, but an emerging option for resilience and optimizing time-of-use energy rates.

- **Wind Turbines:** Rare for individual homes (needs certain conditions, zoning and sufficient wind), but small wind turbines could supplement in rural windy sites.
- **Net Metering:** Many locales allow sending excess solar power back to the grid for credit. Understanding your local policy is part of planning renewables.

C. Efficient Lighting and Appliances:

- By now, LED lighting is standard for new builds, using ~75% less energy than old incandescent and lasting much longer.
- Energy Star rated appliances ensure each fridge, dishwasher, etc., uses less electricity/water.
- Consider induction cooktops instead of gas, they're extremely efficient (and eliminate combustion indoors).
- Smart power strips and home automation to turn off lights or standby power can eke out small savings.

D. Advanced Building Envelope:

- **Structural Insulated Panels (SIPs):** These are prefab panels with insulation sandwiched between OSB boards. They create a very tight, well-insulated wall quickly.
- **Insulated Concrete Forms (ICFs):** Hollow foam blocks that are stacked and filled with concrete, result is a highly insulated, airtight and disaster-resilient wall (ICF houses perform very well in storms). They have high thermal mass and about R-20 to R-25 effective insulation plus the mass effect.
- **Double-stud Walls or Offset Studs:** Creating thicker walls filled entirely with insulation or staggering studs to reduce thermal paths can achieve extremely high R-values (like a 12" thick double-stud wall can be R-40+).

- **Cool Roofs & Attic Venting:** In hot climates, a radiant barrier in the attic or cool roof material can cut AC loads. Solar reflective shingles or a metal roof with reflective coating keeps attics cooler. Adequate venting (ridge + soffit) is important to let built-up heat escape.
- **Windows & Shading:** Beyond picking Energy Star windows, using the right SHGC (solar heat gain coefficient) glass for climate, e.g., lower SHGC in hot climates to reject sun, higher SHGC in cold climates to gain heat. Also incorporate shading like awnings, pergolas, or deciduous trees that block summer sun but allow winter sun through to windows.
- **Air Tightness:** Achieving an airtightness of 1.5 ACH50 or better (which is significantly tighter than code in many places) can save a lot of energy. It requires careful sealing of every penetratio and often a "blower door directed air sealing" approach, or using membranes like AeroBarrier (a mist that seals leaks, used while pressurizing the house) which can get to Passive House levels relatively easily.
- **Thermal Imaging:** Some builders use infrared cameras to spot any missing insulation or leaks to fix them during construction, ensuring the envelope is performing as intended.

Table 8.1, Benefits of Key Sustainable Features

Feature	Benefit	Typical ROI (Return on Investment)
High R-Value Insulation & Air Sealing	Drastically reduced heating/cooling needs; smaller HVAC possible; increased comfort (no drafts)	Medium-High ROI (pays back over years in energy savings; also improves resale value)
Energy-Efficient Windows (Low-E, double/triple pane)	Lower heat loss and gain; less condensation; improved comfort near windows	Medium ROI (savings on bills, especially in extreme climates; also noise reduction value)
Solar PV System (5kW example)	Generates clean electricity ~20-30% of typical home use; protection from future energy price rises	Medium ROI (5-10 year payback in many cases with incentives; then essentially free energy)
Heat Pump Water Heater (Hybrid)	Uses ~1/3 the electricity of a standard electric water heater by extracting heat from air	Medium ROI (few year payback on bills; also can cool/dehumidify space it's in slightly)
Low-Flow Fixtures (WaterSense faucets, dual-flush toilets)	Significant water savings ~20-30% per fixture; lower utility bills; less strain on septic or community supply	High ROI (low cost to implement, immediate ongoing savings on water/heating)
Native/xeriscape landscaping & Rainwater harvesting	Reduced irrigation need (can save thousands of gallons); rain barrels can supply garden water; contributes to stormwater management	Medium ROI (saves on water bills if metered; intangible benefits to environment; rainwater system cost varies)
Recycled/renewable materials (bamboo flooring, recycled countertops, etc.)	Conserves resources; often lower emissions in manufacture; can be marketing point for green home	ROI varies (sometimes cost-neutral choices, other times premium; mainly an environmental ROI rather than direct financial)
Smart Home Energy Monitoring	Real-time data can encourage energy-saving behavior and identify issues (like an HVAC that's running too much)	High ROI (low cost for monitor, can lead to changes that save energy; knowledge is power)

8.4 Sustainable Materials and Waste Reduction

Sustainability isn't just about energy; it's also about materials and construction practices:

- **Locally Sourced Materials:** Using stone, lumber, or other materials from the region reduces transportation energy and supports local economy.
- **Rapidly Renewable Materials:** Like bamboo (grows very fast, used for flooring), cork (renewable bark), straw-bale construction (straw is a byproduct and has high R-value too).
- **Recycled Content:** Many products have recycled versions, composite decking from recycled plastic, cellulose insulation from paper, recycled glass countertops, tiles from recycled content, even insulation made from old denim jeans. Steel roofing or framing contains a lot of recycled steel typically.
- **Certifications:** Look for materials certified by organizations (e.g., lumber that is FSC-certified comes from responsibly managed forests).
- **Construction Waste Management:** Rather than sending everything to the dump, a sustainable project will have dumpsters for recycling metal, wood scraps, cardboard, etc. Perhaps wood cut-offs are chipped for mulch, or excess insulation donated. Planning dimensions can reduce off-cut waste (for example, designing room dimensions to align with 4' increments reduces drywall waste).
- **Durability and Adaptability:** A building that lasts longer and can adapt to new uses is ultimately more sustainable (less frequent need for new materials). That means moisture management (to avoid rot), resilient design for storms, and even things like designing an office that

could become a bedroom easily or a basement that can be finished later , built-in flexibility.

- **Toxicity and Health:** Choose **low-VOC paints and finishes**, avoid products with added formaldehyde (common in some plywood and cabinets, but now you can find no-added-formaldehyde versions). Ensure good ventilation during construction to clear out any off-gassing before occupancy.

8.5 The Future of Sustainable Home Building

We stand at an interesting point in home building. Energy codes are getting stricter, pushing many standard practices towards what used to be "above-and-beyond." For instance, California's 2020 code required solar PV on new houses, and many places are aiming for net-zero ready construction by 2030. **Passive House** standards originating in Germany are influencing higher-performance building globally, showing that a ~90% heating/cooling energy reduction is possible with current tech.

Future homes may increasingly:

a. Use **prefabrication and modular construction** to reduce waste and ensure quality (prefab components can have tighter joints, etc.).

b. Incorporate **smart grids** tech, houses that not only draw power but also supply it back and communicate with the grid to balance loads (your water heater might heat when there's excess solar and pause when grid is strained, for example).

c. Use **battery electric storage and electric vehicles** as part of home energy strategy (your car battery potentially serving as backup power source).

d. Be constructed with **low-carbon materials**: e.g., concrete alternatives or concrete with carbon capture, non-petroleum-based insulation (there's wool, cork, even mushroom mycelium insulation being developed).

e. Emphasize **resilience**: Designing for more intense weather (wind, wildfire-resistant materials, elevated foundations in flood-prone areas, etc.) is also a sustainability aspect, a home that survives disaster doesn't need rebuilding (sparing resources).

f. Provide a comfortable habitat not just for humans but be in harmony with nature, think native landscaping that supports pollinators, rain gardens that manage runoff, even integrating architecture with greenery (like green walls or rooftop gardens).

- **Checklist**: *Green Build Options (for planning), Did we maximize insulation within reason of diminishing returns?; Did we choose at least Energy Star (or better) windows, doors, appliances?; Is the HVAC right-sized (not oversized) and high efficiency?; Are all water fixtures WaterSense rated?; What's the plan for solar, install now or make "solar-ready" (conduit run, space for inverter and future panels)?; Did we use any recycled materials or sustainably sourced options where possible (without breaking budget)?; Are construction waste recycling arrangements made?; Final blower door test and HVAC commissioning done (so the home performs as intended); Have we educated the homeowner on how to use the home efficiently (this is important, even a great system can be defeated by misuse. Simple guidance like filter changes, programming thermostat, etc., ensure the sustainable design translates to sustainable operation).*

- **Homeowner Tip**: *If you're an owner interested in sustainability, involve yourself early. Some features are much easier to put in during construction than later (e.g., wiring for solar or an EV charger, roughing in greywater plumbing). Also look for incentives: governments and utilities often provide rebates or tax credits for solar, insulation upgrades, efficient HVAC, etc. That can substantially offset costs. Living in a green home, you might also notice differences: it may be more airtight, use your ventilation and be mindful of chemicals you bring in (like limit heavy use of chemical cleaners, indoor air quality is in your hands too). You'll likely enjoy lower bills, set some aside, perhaps, for eventual battery storage or future tech upgrades, making your efficient home even more self-sufficient. Finally, take pride that your home is part of the climate solution, it's minimizing waste and pollution while providing a healthy haven for you and your family.*

Homeowner Summary, Sustainable Building: A sustainable, energy-efficient home is essentially about **smart choices**, in design, materials, and equipment. While some choices might cost a bit more upfront, they pay back over time and align with a broader responsibility to the planet and future generations. The result for the homeowner is a house that's comfortable, quiet, and affordable to operate. It's a win-win-win: good for the builder's reputation and craft (building for the future), good for the homeowner's wallet and well-being, and good for the environment. By incorporating even a few sustainable features (and there are many to choose from), you transform a mere structure into a forward-thinking home. The Construction Pyramid stands not just as a testament to strength and longevity, but now also to sustainability, built to last and built to live lightly on the earth.

Chapter 9: Top 10 Construction Mistakes

Even the most well-intentioned builders or enthusiastic homeowners can make mistakes during a construction project, especially if it's a first time experience. Some mistakes cause minor headaches, while others can lead to serious cost overruns or structural issues. In this chapter, we compile the **Top 10 Rookie Mistakes** seen in residential construction, along with actionable advice on how to avoid them. Learning from others' missteps is a lot cheaper and easier than learning from your own! Whether you're managing a build or just overseeing a contractor, being aware of these common pitfalls helps you stay proactive and keep your project on track.

Mistake #1: Poor Planning and Budgeting

What happens: Diving into construction without a detailed plan and budget is like setting sail without a map. New builders often underestimate costs or forget certain expenses (permits, utility hookups, landscaping) in their budget. They may also start building before finalizing design details, leading to changes on the fly that blow the budget.

Avoid it: Invest time in **thorough planning**. Develop a realistic budget with a contingency (at least 10-15% for unexpected items). Do your homework on costs: get multiple quotes for major work, use cost-estimating guides, and consider hiring an architect or professional estimator for complex projects. Plan the project scope and design fully before breaking ground. It's much cheaper to erase a line on a blueprint than to move a wall on site. If you must cut costs, do it in the planning stage by adjusting scope or specs, rather than mid-build panic cuts.

Mistake #2: Skipping Permits or Inspections

What happens: Eager to get started, some may skip pulling the proper building permits or think certain inspections are not important. This can lead to legal troubles, fines, or worse, safety hazards and a house that isn't up to code. Imagine finishing your dream deck only to have the city order it torn down because it wasn't permitted, or discovering too late that an overlooked inspection (like framing or insulation) leads to tearing open walls later.

Avoid it: Always check what permits are required for your project (building, electrical, plumbing, etc.) and obtain them. Schedule the necessary inspections, these are not your enemy, inspectors are there to ensure safety and compliance. If you're DIYing, study the code basics or consult a professional so your work will pass. Keep the paperwork organized, you'll likely need proof of final inspection approvals when you eventually sell the home. Remember, building "under the radar" can cost you far more in the long run than doing it right legally.

Mistake #3: Choosing the Wrong Team (or No Team)

What happens: A rookie might hire the cheapest contractor without thoroughly vetting them, or attempt to DIY tasks well beyond their skill. The wrong contractor could do shoddy work or disappear mid-project. Meanwhile, biting off more than you can chew as an amateur can lead to costly errors or an unfinished house languishing for months/years.

Avoid it: Vet your contractors and subs. Get references, see past work, ensure they are licensed and insured. Don't just take the lowest bid, weigh the reputation and included scope. If acting as an owner-builder, be honest about what you can do vs. what you should leave to pros. It's fine to paint or lay laminate flooring DIY, but maybe bring in experts for structural framing, electrical, or plumbing if you're not trained, those have high stakes for error. If managing the build, consider at least consulting with a project manager or experienced mentor to avoid sequencing mistakes (for example, don't paint before the drywall mud is fully cured, etc.). A solid team will save money overall by doing things right the first time.

Mistake #4: Ignoring Soil and Site Prep

What happens: Perhaps the most invisible-yet-critical step, as noted in our Site Prep chapter, is properly analyzing the soil and preparing the site. Rookies might build on poorly compacted fill or unstable soil without testing, leading to foundation settling or cracking. They might neglect drainage, resulting in a perpetually wet basement or eroded yard.

Avoid it: Do the **geotechnical homework**, soil tests, proper excavation, compaction, and install drainage measures (french drains, footing drains, gutters directing water away, etc.). If your site is low, spend the effort to grade it right or bring in fill and compact it to create a crown for the house to sit on. It's hard to overstate: a solid foundation literally and figuratively underpins your success. If a soil report suggests special footing design or over-excavation and replacement of poor soils, follow that advice. A few thousand now could save tens of thousands later fixing a sinking foundation.

Mistake #5: Overlooking Building Codes and Regulations

What happens: Some first-timers might think codes are just red tape and try to bypass certain requirements, like spacing of electrical outlets, proper egress windows in bedrooms, or the amount of attic insulation. This can lead to unsafe conditions or expensive rework when an appraiser or inspector catches it later. Also, forgetting about HOA rules or deed restrictions (e.g., height limits, setbacks) is a common flub that can halt a project in its tracks.

Avoid it: Educate yourself on **local codes or hire someone who knows them** (architect, experienced builder). Use the code as a baseline, it's there to protect occupants' safety and health. Many code requirements are minimums; meeting or even exceeding them is wise (e.g., putting a bit more insulation than code, or using fire-rated drywall where not required but prudent). Also, if in a governed community, get HOA approvals if needed (better to play nice with them than face a cease-and-desist on your construction because a neighbor complained). In short: better to **build to code** than have to tear out and rebuild parts later to comply.

Mistake #6: Constant Design Changes (Scope Creep)

What happens: The project starts with one plan, but as work goes on, the owner or builder keeps making changes, "Let's move this wall 2 feet," or "Oh, let's add another window here, and maybe upgrade the kitchen cabinets." While some adjustments are inevitable, constant changes disrupt schedules, confuse workers, and blow up budgets. You might end up with mismatched materials, or redoing work that was already done the old way.

Avoid it: Freeze the design as much as possible before construction. If you get new ideas, assess if they can wait as later improvements rather than mid-stream changes. When change is necessary, do it formally, update the plans, inform all trades, adjust budget/schedule clearly. Be cautious of "while you're at it" syndrome: It might seem small to add a light here or extend a porch there, but each has ripple effects. One helpful tip is keep a change log with cost and time impact for each alteration, seeing that running total may give pause to non-essential tweaks. Discipline during the build will get you moved in on time and within budget; cosmetic changes can often be done later if still desired.

Mistake #7: Cutting Corners on Quality for Speed or Cost

What happens: Under pressure to finish faster or cheaper, a novice might skip important steps or buy subpar materials. Examples: not allowing concrete to cure properly before loading it, or using undersized beams, or buying bargain-basement windows that leak air. These shortcuts usually come back to haunt in the form of failures, repairs, or just poor performance (high energy bills, drafts, etc.).

Avoid it: Know where you can save and where you shouldn't. **Structural integrity, moisture protection, and safety systems** (electrical, etc.) are never worth skimping on. Use at least code-grade materials or better. It's okay to find efficiencies, perhaps you use a simpler trim profile to save money, but you still install it correctly with proper paint. Or you opt for mid-range countertops instead of top-tier to save cost, but you don't cheap out on the waterproofing for your shower. A good rule: if it's behind walls or hard to change later (structure, insulation, wiring), go for quality; if it's a surface finish (paint color, light fixture) which you can upgrade later easily, that's where budget options are fine. And never sacrifice the essentials (flashing, rebar, fasteners) because they're out of sight.

Mistake #8: Poor Communication and Documentation

What happens: Construction has many players, owner, contractor, subcontractors, inspectors. Miscommunication can lead to mistakes like a wall being built in the wrong place or an outlet omitted because the electrician had an outdated plan. Also, not documenting changes or agreements can cause disputes, "I thought you were going to do X," "No, we never agreed to that." This can sour relationships and cause delays or cost issues.

Avoid it: Communicate clearly and often. Have regular site meetings if possible, or at least weekly check-ins. Use updated plans, ensure all subs get the latest revisions. When making decisions (like placement of a light or type of tile), confirm in writing (even just text or email) so everyone's on the same page. Keep a project binder or digital folder with all selections, specs, and correspondence. It might feel tedious, but it prevents the "I assumed..." errors. Encourage contractors to ask questions if unsure rather than guess. It's better to pause and clarify than to do something over. A well-communicated project tends to run smoother and with fewer do-overs.

Mistake #9: Neglecting Energy Efficiency and Future Costs

What happens: A rookie might focus only on immediate build costs and aesthetics, ignoring things like insulation, efficiency of HVAC, or future maintenance. They end up with a house that maybe looks good but is drafty, expensive to heat/cool, or has high maintenance exteriors. Or they miss easy opportunities for future-proofing (no conduit for EV charger, no blocking for solar, etc.).

Avoid it: Think **long-term and lifecycle costs**. Spending a bit more on thicker insulation or better windows during construction could pay off every month in utility savings. Choose materials that last (fiber-cement siding over cheap hardboard that rots, for instance). If budget is tight, at least make the home ready for future upgrades, run conduit to an attic or roof for solar panels later, wire a heavy circuit to the garage for an electric car charger even if you don't have one yet, etc. Consider the climate and choose HVAC accordingly, maybe that efficient heat pump will be worth it in a few years of energy savings. Essentially, build not just for today, but for the coming decades. Your future self (or future buyer) will thank you.

Mistake #10: Unrealistic Timeline Expectations

What happens: First-time builders often underestimate how long things take. Perhaps expecting to finish the whole house in 3 months because some TV show did it. This leads to frustration, rushed work (see mistake #7), or issues like trying to install floors before the drywall mud is fully dry (trapping moisture). If you have to be out of a current home by a certain date and the new one isn't ready, that's a major stress.

Avoid it: Work with a **realistic schedule** with some padding. Understand the critical path, some things can overlap, but many must be sequential (can't install drywall before rough-ins, can't do final paint if humidity is too high, etc.). Weather can also delay exterior work, so have buffer time in rainy or winter seasons. It's often said: in construction, **everything takes longer than you think**. So plan for that. Communicate timeline with trades so they can line up, good subs are busy, and if you miss your slot with them, you might wait weeks for the next. If you finish early, great, maybe you saved some interim financing or rent. But if you plan too optimistically and go over, it can cost in stress and money (interest, etc.). Be patient; rushing to meet an arbitrary deadline can result in cutting corners or burning out. A home is a major project, give it the time it needs to be done right.

Wrap-Up of Mistakes: Building a house (or even a small addition) is a complex dance of decisions. Mistakes will happen; the goal is to minimize them and catch them early when they do. The above list is not to scare, but to prepare. By learning these common pitfalls, you're already ahead of the curve. As you carry on with your project, remember a few overarching themes: *plan carefully, communicate clearly, prioritize quality and safety, and stay adaptable.* If something feels off, it probably is, pause and address it. And when in doubt, consult experienced professionals, a quick paid hour of an engineer's or veteran builder's time for advice can save you costly errors. Every mistake avoided is money and time saved, and some lessons learned this way don't have to be learned the hard way.

A well-managed project will not be perfect, but it will be rewarding. As you avoid these rookie mistakes, you pave the way to move from novice to knowledgeable builder. And when you finally cross the finish line, you can proudly say your home (your *Construction Pyramid*, as it were) was built on a foundation of not just concrete, but solid wisdom and care.

Glossary of Key Construction Terms

This glossary defines key terms used throughout the book, as well as other common residential construction terminology, in plain language.

- **Anchor Bolts:** Heavy bolts that secure the wood framing (mudsill) to the concrete foundation. They keep the house from sliding or lifting off the foundation in events like high winds or earthquakes. Installed in wet concrete of the foundation and later bolted tight.
- **Backfill:** The act of refilling excavated soil around a foundation or in utility trenches after installation. Proper backfill (in layers with compaction) is important to support slabs, sidewalks, and prevent foundation movement.
- **Beam:** A structural horizontal member that carries load from joists or rafters across an open span to posts or walls. Often made of wood (like LVL, laminated veneer lumber) or steel (I-beam). For example, a girder beam might run down a basement to support floor joists.
- **Building Envelope:** The outer shell of the building that separates indoor from outdoor, including walls, windows, doors, roof, and foundation. A tight, well-insulated envelope is key to energy efficiency, keeping weather out and comfort in.
- **Circuit (Electrical):** A loop of wiring that starts at the breaker panel and goes out to power devices (outlets, lights) and returns. Each circuit has a breaker that will trip if the load is too high or a short occurs. For example, kitchen outlets might be on a 20A small-appliance circuit.
- **Flashing:** Thin metal or waterproof material installed at transitions and penetrations (roof valleys, around chimneys, windows, doors, deck ledgers) to prevent

water from seeping in. Flashing is overlapped shingle-style to lead water out and over the exterior surface.

- **Footing:** The lowest part of a foundation system, usually concrete, that spreads the building's load to the soil. For instance, under each foundation wall or column there is a wider footing. Think of it as the "foot" that the structure stands on.
- **Furring Strip:** A thin strip of wood or metal (often 1x3 or similar) used to create a gap or even out a surface. For example, furring strips can be applied to a masonry wall to attach drywall, or on ceilings to create a space for electrical or to level before finishing.
- **HVAC:** Stands for Heating, Ventilation, and Air Conditioning, the systems providing climate control and air circulation in a building. Includes furnace or heat pump, AC unit, ductwork, filters, and fans.
- **Joist:** A horizontal framing member, typically repeated in series, that supports floors or ceilings. For example, floor joists support the subfloor and loads above, running between beams or walls. Commonly made of dimensional lumber (2x8, 2x10) or engineered wood (I-joists).
- **King Stud:** In wall framing, a full-height stud that supports a header at door or window openings. If you imagine a window rough opening, the king studs run from bottom plate to top plate on each side of the opening, providing strength and anchoring the header which sits atop the shorter trimmer/jack studs.
- **Live Load / Dead Load:** Dead load is the weight of the building itself (structure, materials, permanent fixtures). Live load is the weight of temporary forces, people, furniture, snow on a roof, etc. Structures are designed to hold both (e.g., a floor may be designed for 40 pounds per sq ft live load in a living room).

- **Mudsill (Sill Plate):** The bottom horizontal wood member that sits on the foundation (anchored by anchor bolts). The rest of the wall framing attaches to it. It's usually pressure-treated wood to resist decay since it's in contact with masonry.
- **R-Value:** A measure of thermal resistance (how well a material insulates). Higher R-value means better insulation. For example, 3.5" of fiberglass batt might be R-13, whereas 2" of extruded polystyrene foam might be R-10. Building codes specify minimum R-values for different parts of the home.
- **Sheathing:** Panels (plywood, OSB, or boards) that cover the exterior of walls, floors, and roofs, onto which other materials (siding, roofing) are attached. Sheathing adds rigidity (shear strength) and forms part of the building envelope. Example: 1/2" OSB wall sheathing under siding.
- **Span:** The distance a framing member travels between supports. For instance, a steel beam might span 20 feet between columns, or a joist might span 12 feet between a wall and a beam. Span tables determine allowable spans based on material and load.
- **Subfloor:** The structural floor layer directly on floor joists, typically plywood or OSB panels, which is then covered by underlayment or finish flooring. The subfloor ties joists together and provides a base for carpet, wood, tile, etc.
- **Thermal Bridge:** An area of an object which has higher thermal conductivity than the surrounding materials, creating a path of least resistance for heat transfer. In houses, wood studs are a thermal bridge through insulation (since wood is less insulative), allowing more heat loss. Solutions include adding continuous insulation over studs to break the bridge.

- **Tongue and Groove (T&G):** A way of joining boards or panels where one has a protruding "tongue" side and the other a "groove" side so they interlock. Common in wood flooring, wall paneling, and subfloor sheets. It helps prevent one board from moving up/down relative to next, giving a smooth surface.
- **Truss:** A pre-engineered structural assembly, usually triangular in shape for roofs or sometimes floor systems, that uses smaller lumber pieces in a web to span large distances. Roof trusses often allow quick installation and can span longer than simple rafters. They come as single piece units delivered to site.
- **Vapor Barrier / Vapor Retarder:** A material that slows or stops the diffusion of water vapor through walls or ceilings. Often a plastic sheet or special paint. Placed typically on the warm side of insulation (inside in cold climates, outside in hot humid climates, or sometimes none in mixed climates) to prevent moisture from condensing inside walls. Modern term "vapor retarder" is used as it's rarely an impermeable barrier but rather something with limited permeability.
- **Walkthrough (Final Walkthrough):** A last inspection of the completed project, usually with the owner and contractor, to note any issues that need fixing (touch-ups, repairs) and to ensure everything is done as agreed before handover. Also a time for demonstrating how systems work, locating shutoffs, etc.
- **Zoning (HVAC & Planning):** Two meanings, in HVAC, zoning means dividing the home's HVAC system into independently controlled areas. In land-use, zoning refers to local regulations dictating what, where, and how you can build on a property (residential, commercial, setbacks, height limits, etc.). Both kinds of zoning critically impact residential construction planning.

Last point:

By weaving together all these chapters, from the first spade in the ground to the last drop of paint, **Construction Pyramid: Technical Knowledge You Must Know for Residential Construction** has aimed to equip you with both the big-picture understanding and the nitty-gritty details of home building. We balanced the technical accuracy with accessible language, added real-world case studies to ground the concepts, and integrated handy tables, checklists, and tips so you can readily apply the knowledge. Whether you're a prospective homeowner about to embark on building your dream house, a student of construction, or a budding contractor, we hope this comprehensive guide demystifies the process and instills confidence.

Building a house is a grand journey. It can feel overwhelming with so many moving parts, but remember that every expert builder was once a rookie, every sturdy house started as a hole in the ground, and every challenge has a solution. With careful planning, the right knowledge (now at your fingertips), and a bit of perseverance, you can turn that patch of dirt into a **home built to last**, just like the enduring Construction Pyramid of our metaphor.

Happy Building, may your foundations be strong, your walls plumb, and your spirit undaunted. Here's to the house that becomes a home and the builder that grows with each brick laid!

References

Alrwashdeh, S. S. (2023). Energy profit evaluation of a photovoltaic system from a selected building in Jordan. *Results in Engineering, 18*, 101177. https://doi.org/10.1016/j.rineng.2023.101177

Jonnala, S. N., Gogoi, D., Devi, S., Kumar, M., & Kumar, C. (2024). A comprehensive study of building materials and bricks for residential construction. *Construction and Building Materials, 425*, 135931. https://doi.org/10.1016/j.conbuildmat.2024.135931

Naghibalsadati, F., Gitifar, A., Ray, S., Richter, A., & Ng, K. T. W. (2024). Temporal evolution and thematic shifts in sustainable construction and demolition waste management through building information modeling technologies: A text-mining analysis. *Journal of Environmental Management, 369*, 122293. https://doi.org/10.1016/j.jenvman.2024.122293

Naghibalsadati, F., Gitifar, A., Richter, A., Tasnim, A., & Ng, K. T. W. (2025). Uncovering key themes in modular construction waste management and exploring their impact and centrality. *Results in Engineering*, 104550. https://doi.org/10.1016/j.rineng.2025.104550

Rajala, P., Ylä-Kujala, A., Sinkkonen, T., & Kärri, T. (2022). Profitability in construction: How does building renovation business fare compared to new building business. *Construction Management and Economics, 40*(3), 223–237. https://doi.org/10.1080/01446193.2022.2032228

Ray, S., Ng, K. T. W., Mahmud, T. S., Richter, A., & Naghibalsadati, F. (2024). Quantification of construction and demolition waste disposal behaviors during COVID-19 using satellite imagery. *Environmental and Sustainability Indicators, 24*, 100502. https://doi.org/10.1016/j.indic.2024.100502

Sammour, F., Alkailani, H., Sweis, G. J., Sweis, R. J., Maaitah, W., & Alashkar, A. (2023). Forecasting demand in the residential construction industry using machine learning algorithms in Jordan. *Construction Innovation, 24*(5), 1228–1254. https://doi.org/10.1108/ci-10-2022-0279

107

Made in the USA
Coppell, TX
31 July 2025

52558404R00069